Seasonable Counsel, or, Advice to Sufferers

By: John Bunyan

John Bunyan

1628-1688

INTRODUCTION

John Bunyan (28 November 1628 – 31 August 1688) was an English Christian writer and preacher, famous for writing The Pilgrim's Progress. Though he was a Reformed Baptist, in the Church of England he is remembered with a Lesser Festival on 30 August, and on the liturgical calendar of the Episcopal Church (USA) on August 29. As his popularity and notoriety grew, Bunyan increasingly became a target for slander and libel; he was described as "a witch, a Jesuit, a highwayman" and was said to have mistresses and multiple wives.

In 1658, aged 30, he was arrested for preaching at Eaton Socon and indicted for preaching without a licence. He continued preaching, however, and did not suffer imprisonment until November 1660, when he was taken to the County gaol in Silver Street, Bedford. In that same year, Bunyan married his second wife, Elizabeth, by whom he had two more children, Sarah and Joseph. The Restoration of the monarchy by Charles II of England began Bunyan's persecution as England returned to Anglicanism. Meeting-houses were quickly closed and all citizens were required to attend their Anglican parish church. It became punishable by law to "conduct divine service except in accordance with the ritual of the church, or for one not in Episcopal orders to address a congregation." Thus, John Bunyan no longer had that freedom to preach which he had enjoyed under the Puritan Commonwealth. He was arrested on 12 November 1660, whilst preaching privately in Lower Samsell by Harlington, Bedfordshire, 10 miles south of Bedford.

Bunyan in prison

Bunyan's home

Bunyan in prison

Bunyan preaching

Bust of Bunyan

TO THE CHRISTIAN READER

BELOVED, I thought it convenient, since many at this day are exposed to sufferings, to give my advice touching that to thee. Namely, that thou wouldest take heed to thyself, and keep thy soul diligently, and not suffer thyself to be entangled in those snares that God hath suffered to be laid in the world for some. Beware of "men" in the counsel of Christ "for they will deliver you up" (Matt 10:17). Keep thou therefore within the bounds of uprightness and integrity towards both God and man: for that will fortify, that will preserve thee, if not from, yet under the rage of men, in a comfortable and quiet frame of heart. Wherefore do that, and that only, that will justify thy innocency, and that will help thee, not with forced speech, but with good conscience, when oppressed, to make thy appeals to God, and to the consciences of all men.

This is the advice that, I thank God, I have taken myself: for I find that there is nothing, next to God and his grace by Christ, that can stand one in such stead, as will a good and harmless conscience.

I hope I can say that God has made me a Christian: and a Christian must be a harmless man, and to that end, must embrace nothing but harmless principles. A Christian's business, as a Christian, is to believe in Jesus Christ, and in God the Father by him; and to seek the good of all about him, according as his place, state and capacity in this world will admit, not meddling with other men's matters, but ever following that which is good.
A Christian is a child of the kingdom of God, and that kingdom, take it as it begins in grace, or as it is perfected in glory, is not of this world but of that which is to come: and though men of old, as some may now, be afraid of that kingdom: yet that kingdom will hurt no man, neither with its principles, nor by itself. To instance somewhat, Faith in Christ: what harm can that do? A life regulated by a moral law, what hurt is in that? Rejoicing in spirit for the hope of the life to come by Christ, who will that harm? Nor is the instituted worship of our Lord of any evil tendency, Christianity teaches us also to do our enemies good, to "Bless them that hate us, and to pray for them that despitefully use us and persecute us," and what evil can be in that? This is the sum of the Christian religion, as by the word may be plainly made appear: wherefore I counsel thee to keep close to these things, and touch with nothing that jostleth therewith.

Nor do thou marvel, thou living thus, if some should be so foolish as to seek thy hurt, and to afflict thee, because thy works are good (1 John 3:12,13). For there is need that thou shouldest at sometimes be in manifold temptations, thy good and innocent life notwithstanding (1 Peter 1:6). For, to omit other things, there are some of the graces of God that are in thee, that as to some of their acts, cannot shew themselves, nor their excellency, nor their power, nor what they can do: but as thou art in a suffering state. Faith and patience, in persecution, has that to do, that to shew, and that to perform, that cannot be done, shewed, nor performed any where else but there. There is also a patience of hope; a rejoicing in hope, when we are in tribulation, that is, over and above that which we have when we are at ease and quiet. That also that all graces can endure, and triumph over, shall not be known, but when, and as we are in a state of affliction. Now these acts of our graces are of that worth and esteem with God, also he so much delighteth in them: that occasion through his righteous judgment, must be ministered for them to shew their beauty, and what bravery there is in them.

It is also to be considered that those acts of our graces, that cannot be put forth, or shew themselves in their splendour, but when we Christianly suffer, will yield such fruit to those whose trials call them to exercise, that will, in the day of God, abound to their comfort, and tend to their perfection in glory (1 Peter 1:7; 2 Cor 4:17).

Why then should we think that our innocent lives will exempt us from sufferings, or that troubles shall do us such harm? For verily it is for our present and future good that our God doth send them upon us. I count therefore, that such things are necessary for the health of our souls, as bodily pains and labour are for [the health of] the body. People that live high, and in idleness, bring diseases upon the body: and they that live in all fullness of gospel-ordinances, and are not exercised with trials, grow gross, are diseased and full of bad humours in their souls. And though this may to some seem strange: yet our day has given us such an experimental proof of the truth thereof, as has not been known for some ages past.

Alas! we have need of those bitter pills, at which we so winch and shuck: and it will be well if at last we be purged as we should thereby. I am sure we are but little the better as yet, though the physician has had us so long in hand. Some bad humours may possibly ere long be driven out: but at present the disease is so high, that it makes some professors fear more a consumption will be made in their purses by these doses, than they desire to be made better in their souls thereby. I see that I still have need of these trials; and if God will by these judge me as he judges his saints, that I may not be condemned with the world, I will cry, Grace, grace for ever. The consideration also that we have deserved these things, much silences me as to what may yet happen unto me. I say, to think that we have deserved them of God, though against men we have done nothing, makes me lay my hand upon my mouth, and causes me to hold my tongue. Shall we deserve correction? And be angry because we have it! Or shall it come to save us? and shall we be offended with the hand that brings it! Our sickness is so great that our enemies take notice of it; let them know too that we also take our purges patiently. We are willing to pay for those potions that are given us for the health of our body, how sick soever they make us: and if God will have us pay too for that which is to better our souls, why should we grudge thereat? Those that bring us these medicines have little enough for their pains: for my part, I profess, I would not for a great deal, be bound, for their wages, to do their work. True, physicians are for the most part chargeable, and the niggards are too loth to part with their money to them: but when necessity says they must either take physic, or die: of two evils they desire to choose the least. Why, affliction is better than sin, and if God sends the one to cleanse us from the other, let us thank him, and be also content to pay the messenger.

And thou that art so loth to pay for thy sinning, and for the means that puts thee upon that exercise of thy graces, as will be for thy good hereafter: take heed of tempting of God lest he doubleth this potion unto thee. The child, by eating of raw fruit, stands in need of physic, but the child of a childish humour refuseth to take the potion, what follows but a doubling of the affliction, to wit, frowns, chides, and further threatenings and a forcing of the bitter pills upon him. But let me, to persuade thee to lie down and take thy potion, tell thee, it is of absolute necessity, to wit, for thy spiritual and internal health. For, First, Is it better that thou receive judgment in this world, or that thou stay for it to be condemned with the ungodly in the next? Second, Is it better that thou shouldest, as to some acts of thy graces, be foreign, and a stranger, and consequently that thou shouldest lose that far more exceeding, and eternal weight of glory that is prepared as the reward thereof? or that thou shouldest receive it at the hand of God, when the day shall come that every man shall have praise of him for their doings? Third, And I say again, since chastisements are a sign of sonship, a token of love: and the contrary a sign of bastardy, and a token of hatred (Heb 12:6-8; Hosea 4:14). Is it not better that we bear those tokens and marks in our flesh that bespeak us to belong to Christ, than those that declare us to be none of his? For my part, God help me to choose rather to suffer affliction with the people of God, than to enjoy the pleasures of sin for a season: and God of his mercy prepare me for his will.

I am not for running myself into sufferings, but if godliness will expose me to them, the Lord God make me more godly still: for I believe there is a world to come. But, Christian reader, I would not detain thee from a sight of those sheets in thy hand: only let me beg of thee, that thou wilt not be offended either with God, or men, if the cross is laid heavy upon thee. Not with God, for he doth nothing without a cause, nor with men, for they are the hand of God: and will they, nill they; they are the servants of God to thee for good (Psa 17:14; Jer 24:5). Take therefore what comes to thee from God by them, thankfully. If the messenger that brings it is glad that it is in his power to do thee hurt, and to afflict thee; if he skips for joy at thy calamity: be sorry for him; pity him, and pray to thy Father for him: he is ignorant and understandeth not the judgment of thy God, yea he sheweth by this his behavior, that though he, as God's ordinance, serveth thee by afflicting of thee: yet means he nothing less than to destroy thee: by the which also he prognosticates before thee that he is working out his own damnation by doing of thee good. Lay therefore the woeful state of such to heart, and render him that which is good for his evil; and love for his hatred to thee; then shalt thou shew that thou art acted by a spirit of holiness, and art like thy heavenly Father. And be it so, that thy pity and prayers can do such an one no good, yet they must light some where, or return again, as ships come loaden from the Indies, full of blessings into thine own bosom.

And besides all this, is there nothing in dark providences, for the sake of the sight and observation of which, such a day may be rendered lovely, when it is upon us? Is there nothing of God, of his wisdom and power and goodness to be seen in thunder, and lightning, in hailstones? in storms? and darkness and tempests? Why then is it said, he "hath his way in the whirlwind and in the storm" (Nahum 1:3). And why have God's servants of old made such notes, and observed from them such excellent and wonderful things. There is that of God to be seen in such a day as cannot be seen in another. His power in holding up some, his wrath in leaving of others; his making of shrubs to stand, and his suffering of cedars to fall; his infatuating of the counsels of men, and his making of the devil to outwit himself; his giving of his presence to his people, and his leaving of his foes in the dark; his discovering the uprightness of the hearts of his sanctified ones, and laying open the hypocrisy of others, is a working of spiritual wonders in the day of his wrath and of the whirlwind and storm.

These days! these days are the days that do most aptly give an occasion to Christians, of any, to take the exactest measures and scantlings of ourselves. We are apt to overshoot, in days that are calm, and to think ourselves far higher, and more strong than we find we be, when the trying day is upon us. The mouth of Gaal and the boasts of Peter were great and high before the trial came, but when that came, they found themselves to fall far short of the courage they thought they had (Judg 9:38). We also, before the temptation comes, think we can walk upon the sea, but when the winds blow, we feel ourselves begin to sink. Hence such a time is rightly said to be a time to try us, or to find out what we are, and is there no good in this? Is it not this that rightly rectifies our judgment about ourselves, that makes us to know ourselves, that tends to cut off those superfluous sprigs of pride and self-conceitedness, wherewith we are subject to be overcome? Is not such a day, the day that bends us, humbleth us, and that makes us bow before God, for our faults committed in our prosperity? and yet doth it yield no good unto us? we cold not live without such turnings of the hand of God upon us. We should be overgrown with flesh, if we had not our seasonable winters. It is said that in some countries trees will grow, but will bear no fruit, because there is no winter there. The Lord bless all seasons to his people, and help them rightly to behave themselves, under all the times that go over them.
Farewell. I am thine to serve thee in the gospel,

JOHN BUNYAN.

ADVICE TO SUFFERERS

"WHEREFORE LET THEM THAT SUFFER ACCORDING TO THE WILL OF GOD, COMMIT THE KEEPING OF THEIR SOULS TO HIM IN WELL DOING, AS UNTO A FAITHFUL CREATOR"—1 PETER 4:19.

This epistle was written to saints in affliction, specially those of the circumcision, for whom this

Peter was an apostle. And it was written to them to counsel, and comfort them in their affliction. To counsel them as to the cause, for which they were in afflictions, and as to the right management of themselves, and their cause, under their affliction. To comfort them also both with respect to their present help from God, and also with reference to the reward that (they faithfully continuing to the end) should of God be bestowed upon them: all which we shall have occasion, more distinctly, to handle in this following discourse.

The text is a conclusion, drawn from the counsel and comfort which the apostle had afore given them in their suffering state. As who should say, my brethren, as you are now afflicted, so sufferings are needful for you, and therefore profitable and advantageous: wherefore be content to bear them. And that you may indeed bear them with such Christian contentedness, and patience as becomes you; commit the keeping of your souls to your God as unto a faithful Creator. "Let them that suffer according to the will of God, commit the keeping of their souls to him [in well doing,] as unto a faithful Creator."

In this conclusion, therefore, we have three things very fit for sufferers to concern themselves with. FIRST, A direction to a duty of absolute necessity. SECOND, A description of the persons, who are unto this, so necessary a duty, directed. THIRD, An insinuation of the good effect that will certainly follow to those that after a due manner shall take this blessed advice.

The duty so absolutely necessary is, that sufferers "commit the keeping of their souls to God." The sufferers here intended, are those "that suffer according to the will of God." The good insinuated, that will be the effect of our true doing of this, is, we shall find God "a faithful Creator."

[FIRST—THE DUTY TO WHICH SUFFERERS ARE DIRECTED.]

We will first begin with the duty, that sufferers are here directed to, namely, the committing of their souls to God. "Let them - commit the keeping of their souls to him, in well doing."

And I find two things in it that first call for explaining before I proceed. 1. What we must here understand by "the soul." 2. What by "committing" the soul to God.

1. For the first: "The soul," here, is to be taken for that most excellent part of man, that dwelleth in the body; that immortal, spiritual substance, that is, and will be capable of life, and motion, of sense and reason; yea, that will abide a rational being, when the body is returned to the dust as it was. This is that great thing, that our Lord Jesus intends, when he bids his disciples in a day of trial, fear him that can destroy both body and soul in hell (Luke 12:5). That great thing, I say, that he there cautions them to take care of. According to Peter here, "Let them commit the keeping of their soul to him in well doing."

2. Now to "commit" this soul to God, is to carry it to him, to lift it to him, upon my bended

knees, and to pray him for the Lord Jesus Christ's sake, to take it into his holy care, and to let it be under his keeping. Also, that he will please to deliver it from all those snares that are laid for it, betwixt this and the next world, and that he will see that it be forthcoming, safe and sound, at the great and terrible judgment, notwithstanding so many have engaged themselves against it. Thus David committed his soul to God, when he said "Arise, O Lord, disappoint him, cast him down: deliver my soul, O Lord, from the wicked, which is thy sword" (Psa 17:13). And again, "Be pleased, O Lord, to deliver me: O Lord, make hast to help me. Let them be ashamed and confounded together that seek after my soul to destroy it" (Psa 40:13,14).

Thus, I have shewed you what the soul is, and what it is to commit the soul to God. This then is the duty that the apostle here exhorteth the sufferers to, namely, to carry their soul to God, and leave it with him while they engage for his name in the world. Now from the apostle's exhortation to this great duty, I will draw these following conclusions.

Conclusion First, That when persecution is raised against a people, there is a design laid for the ruin of those people's souls. This, I say, doth naturally follow from the exhortation. Why else, need they to commit the keeping of their souls to God. For by this word, "Unto God to keep them," is suggested; there is that would destroy them, and that therefore persecution is raised against them. I am not so uncharitable, as to think, that persecuting men design this. But I verily believe that the devil doth design this, when he stirs them up to so sorry a work. In times of trial, says Peter, "your adversary the devil walketh about as a roaring lion, seeking whom he may devour" (1 Peter 5:8).

Alas! men in their acts of this nature, have designs that are lower, and of a more inferior rank. Some of them look no higher than revenge upon the carcass; than the spoiling of their neighbour of his estate, liberty, or life; than the greatening of themselves in this world, by the ruins of those that they have power to spoil. Their "possessors slay them, and hold themselves not guilty: and they that sell them say, Blessed be the Lord, for I am rich" (Zech 11:5).

Ay! But Satan will not be put off thus: it is not a bag of money, or the punishing of the carcass of such a people, that will please or satisfy him. It is the soul that he aims at; the ruin of the precious soul that he hath bent himself to bring to pass. It is this therefore that Peter here hath his heart concerned with. As, who should say, My brethren, are you troubled and persecuted for your faith? look to it, the hand of Satan is in this thing, and whatever men drive at by doing as they do, the devil designs no less than the damnation of your souls. Ware hawk, saith the falconer, when the dogs are coming near her: especially if she be too much minding of her belly, and too forgetful of what the nature of the dog is. Beware Christian, take heed Christian; the devil is desirous to have thee. And who could better give this exhortation than could Peter himself. Who for not taking heed as to this very thing, had like by the devil to have been swallowed up alive: as is manifest to them that heedfully read, and consider how far he was gone, when that persecution was raised against his Master (Luke 22).

When a tyrant goes to dispossess a neighbouring prince of what is lawfully his own: the men that he employeth at arms to overcome, and get the land, they fight for half-crowns, and the like, and are content with their wages: But the tyrant is for the kingdom, nothing will serve him but the kingdom. This is the case: Men when they persecute, are for the stuff, but the devil is for the soul, nor will any thing less than that satisfy him. Let him then that is a sufferer "commit the keeping of his soul to God:" lest stuff, and soul, and all be lost at once.

Conclusion Second, A second conclusion that followeth upon these words, is this: That sufferers, if they have not a care, may be too negligent as to the securing of their souls with God, even when persecution is upon them. For these words, as they are an instruction, so they are an awakening instruction; they call as to people in danger; as to people, not so aware of the danger; or as unto a people that forget, too much, that their souls, and the ruin of them, are sought after by Satan, when trouble attends them for the gospel sake. As, who should say, when troubles are upon you for the gospel's sake, then take heed that you forget not to commit your souls to the keeping of God. We are naturally apt with that good man Gideon, to be threshing out our wheat, that we may hide it from the Midianites (Judg 6:11). But we are not so naturally apt to be busying ourselves to secure our souls with God. The reason is, for that we are more

flesh than spirit, and because the voice of the world makes a bigger sound in our carnal mind, than the word of God doth. Wherefore Peter, here, calls upon us as upon men of forgetful minds, saying, Let them that suffer according to the will of God, have a care of their souls, and take heed, that the fears of the loss of a little of this world, do not make them forget the fear of the losing of their souls. That sufferers are subject to this, may appear by the stir and bustle that at such a time they make to lock all up safe that the hand of man can reach, while they are cold, chill, remiss, and too indifferent about the committing of their soul to God to keep it. This is seen also, in that many, in a time of trouble for their profession, will study more to deceive themselves by a change of notions, by labouring to persuade their consciences to admit them to walk more at large, by hearkening to opinions that please and gratify the flesh, by adhering to bad examples, and taking evil counsels, than they will to make straight steps for their feet: and to commit the keeping of their souls to God. What shall I say, have there not been many, that so long as peace has lasted, have been great swaggerers for religion, who yet so soon as the sun has waxed warm, have flagged, have been discontented, offended, and turned away from him that speaketh from heaven? All which is because men are naturally apt to be more concerned for their goods, carnal peace, and a temporal life, than they are about securing of their souls with God. Wherefore I say, these words are spoken to awaken us to the consideration of soul-concerns, and how that should be safely lodged under the care, protection, and mercy of God, by our committing of it to him, for that purpose, by Jesus Christ our Lord.

Conclusion Third, Another conclusion that followeth upon this exhortation, is this: That persecution doth, sometimes, so hotly follow God's people, as to leave them nothing but a soul to care for. They have had no house, no land, no money, no goods, no life, no liberty, left them to care for. ALL IS GONE BUT THE SOUL. Goods have been confiscated, liberty has been in irons, the life condemned, the neck in a halter, or the body in the fire. So then all, to such, has been gone, and they have had nothing left them to care for, but their soul. "Let them commit the keeping of their soul to God." This conclusion, I say, doth naturally flow from the words. For that the apostle here doth make mention only of the soul, as of that which is left, as of that which yet remains to the sufferer of all that ever he had. Thus they served Christ; they left him nothing but his soul to care for. Thus they served Stephen; they left him nothing but his soul to care for, and they both cared for that, "Father, into thy hands I commend my spirit," said Jesus (Luke 23:46). And "Lord Jesus, receive my spirit," said Stephen (Acts 7:59). As for all other things, they were gone. They parted the very clothes of Christ among themselves before his face, even while he did hang pouring out his life before them, upon the tree. "They parted my garments among them," said he, "and upon my vesture did they cast lots" (Matt 27:35; Mark 15:24; John 19:24). This also has oftentimes been the condition of later Christians, all has been gone, they have been stripped of all, nothing has been left them but "soul" to care for. Job said that he had escaped with the skin of his teeth; and that is but a little: but he doth not escape with so much, that loses all that he has, life and all, we now except the soul. But,

Conclusion Fourth, Another thing that followeth from the words is this; namely, That when the devil and wicked men have done what they could, in their persecuting of the godly; they have yet had their souls at their own dispose. They have not been able to rob them of their souls, they are not able to hurt their souls. The soul is not in their power to touch, without the leave of God, and of him whose soul it is. "And fear not them," saith Christ, "which kill the body, but are not able to kill the soul" (Matt 10:28). This, I say, lies clear also in the text; for the exhortation supposes, that whatever the sufferers, there made mention of, had lost, they had yet their souls at their own dispose. Let them that suffer, even to the loss of goods, liberty, or life, "commit the keeping of their souls to God." As, who should say, though the enemy hath reached them to their all, and stripped them of their all, yet I know, that their soul is not among that all: For their soul is yet free from them, at liberty, and may be disposed of, even as the sufferer will. Wherefore, let him commit the keeping of his soul to God, lest he also through his negligence or carelessness be also spoiled of that. The sufferer, therefore, hath his soul at his own dispose, he may give that away to God Almighty, in spite of all that the devil and the world can do. He may, indeed, see men parting his land, his household stuff, yea, his very raiment among themselves, but they cannot so dispose of his soul. They "have no more that they can do" (Luke 12:4).

Conclusion Fifth, Another conclusion that followeth from these words is this, That a man, when he is a sufferer, is not able to secure his own soul from the hand of hell by any other means, but by the committing of the keeping thereof to God. Do you suffer? Are you in affliction for your profession? Then keep not your soul in your own hand, for fear of losing that with the rest. For no man "can keep alive his own soul" (Psa 22:29). No, not in the greatest calm; no, not when the lion is asleep: how then should he do it at such a time, when the horrible blast of the terrible ones shall beat against his wall. The consideration of this was that that made holy Paul, who was a man upon whom persecution continually attended, commit his soul to God (Acts 20:22-24; 2 Tim 1:12). God, as I shall shew you by and by, is he, and he alone that is able to keep the soul, and deliver it from danger. Man is naturally a self-deceiver, and therefore is not to be trusted, any farther than as the watchful eye of God is over him. But as to his soul, he is not to be trusted with that at all, that must be wholly committed to God, left altogether with him; laid at his feet, and he also must take the charge thereof, or else it is gone, will be lost, and will perish for ever and ever. Wherefore it is a dangerous thing for a man that is a sufferer, to be a senseless man, as to the danger that his soul is in, and a prayerless man, as to the committing of the keeping of it to God. For he that is such, has yet his soul, and the keeping thereof, in his own deceitful hand. And so has he also that stays himself upon his friends, upon his knowledge, the promise of men, or the mercy of his enemies, or that has set in his mind a bound to himself, how far he will venture for religion, and where he will stop. This is the man that makes not God his trust, and that therefore will surely fall in the day of his temptation. Satan, who now hunteth for the precious soul to destroy it, has power, as well as policy, beyond what man can think. He has power to blind, harden, and to make insensible, the heart. He also can make truth in the eyes of the suffering man, a poor, little, and insignificant thing. Judas had not committed the keeping of his soul to God, but abode in himself, and was left in his tabernacle: and you by and by see what a worthy price he set upon himself, his Christ, and heaven, and all. All to him was not now worth thirty pieces of silver.

And as he can make truth in thy esteem to be little, so he can make sufferings great, and ten times more terrible, than he that hath committed the keeping of his soul to God shall ever find them. A jail shall look as black as hell, and the loss of a few stools and chairs, as bad as the loss of so many bags of gold. Death for the Saviour of the world, shall seem to be a thing both unreasonable and intolerable. Such will choose to run the hazard of the loss of a thousand souls, in the way of the world, rather than the loss of one poor, sorry, transitory life for the holy Word of God. But the reason, as I said, is, they have not committed the keeping of their soul to God. For he that indeed has committed the keeping of his soul to that great one, has shaken his hands of all things here. Has bid adieu to the world, to friends, and life: and waiteth upon God in a way of close keeping to his truth, and walking in his ways, having counted the cost, and been persuaded to take what cup God shall suffer the world to give him for so doing.

Conclusion Sixth, Another conclusion that followeth from these words, is, That God is very willing to take the charge and care of the soul (that is committed unto him) of them that suffer for his sake in the world. If this were not true, the exhortation would not answer the end. What is intended by, "Let him commit the keeping of his soul to God," but that the sufferer should indeed leave that great care with him; but if God be not willing to be concerned with such a charge, what bottom is there for the exhortation? But the exhortation has this for its bottom, therefore God is willing to take the charge and care of the soul of him that suffereth for his name in this world. "The Lord redeemeth the soul of his servants: and none of them that trust in him shall be desolate" (Psa 34:22; 1 Sam 25:28,29). None, not one that committeth his soul to God's keeping in a way of well doing, but shall find him willing to be concerned therewith.

Ay, this, saith the sufferer, if I could believe this, it would rid me of all my fears. But I find myself engaged for God, for I have made a profession of his name, and cannot arrive to this belief that God is willing to take the charge and care of my soul. Wherefore I fear, that if trials come so high, as that life, as well as estate, must go, that both life, and estate, and soul, and all will be lost at once.

Well, honest heart, these are thy fears, but let them fly away, and consider the text again, Let them that suffer according to the will of God, commit the keeping of their souls to him, - as unto a faithful Creator." These are God's words, Christ's words, and the invitation of the Holy Ghost. When, therefore, thou readest them, be persuaded that thou hearest the Father, and the Son, and the Holy Ghost, all of them jointly and severally speaking to thee and saying, Poor sinner, thou art engaged for God in the world, thou art suffering for his Word: leave thy soul with him as with one that is more willing to save it, than thou art willing he should: act faith, trust God, believe his Word, and go on in thy way of witness-bearing for him, and thou shalt find all well, and according to the desire of thy heart at last. True, Satan will make it his business to tempt thee to doubt of this, that thy way be made yet more hard and difficult to thee. For he knows that unbelief is a soul-perplexing sin, and makes that which would otherwise be light, pleasant, and easy, unutterably heavy and burdensome to the sufferer. Yea, this he doth in hope to make thee at last, to cast away thy profession, thy cause, thy faith, thy conscience, thy soul, and all. But hear what the Holy Ghost saith again: "He shall spare the poor and needy, and shall save the souls of the needy. He shall redeem their soul from deceit and violence: and precious shall their blood be in his sight" (Psa 72:13,14). These words also are spoken for the comfort of sufferers, ver. 12. "For he shall deliver the needy when he crieth; the poor also, and him that hath no helper." Wherefore, let them that are God's sufferers, pluck up a good heart; let them not be afraid to trust God with their souls, and with their eternal concerns. Let them cast all their care upon God, for he careth for them (1 Peter 5:7).

But I am in the dark.

I answer, never stick at that. It is most bravely done, to trust God with my soul in the dark, and to resolve to serve God for nothing, rather than give out. Not to see, and yet to believe, and to be a follower of the Lamb, and yet to be at uncertainty, what we shall have at last, argues love, fear, faith, and an honest mind, and gives the greatest sign of one that hath true sincerity in his soul. It was this that made Job and Peter so famous, and the want of it that took away much of the glory of the faith of Thomas (Job 1:8-10,21; Matt 19:27; John 20:29). Wherefore believe, verily, that

God is ready, willing, yea, that he looks for, and expects that thou who art a sufferer shouldest commit the keeping of thy soul to him, as unto a faithful Creator.

Conclusion Seventh. Another conclusion that followeth from these words is this, namely, That God is able, as well as willing, to secure the souls of his suffering saints, and to save them from the evil of all their trials, be they never so many, divers, or terrible. "Let him commit the keeping of his soul to God," but to what boot, if he be not able to keep it in his hand, and from the power of him that seeks the soul to destroy it? But "my Father which gave them me," saith Christ, "is greater than all; and no man is able to pluck them out of my Father's hand" (John 10:29). So then there can be no sorrow, affliction, or misery invented, by which the devil may so strongly prevail, as thereby to pluck the soul out of the hand of him who has received it, to keep it from falling, and perishing thereby. The text therefore supposeth a sufficiency of power in God to support, and a sufficiency of comfort and goodness to embolden the soul to endure for him: let Satan break out, and his instruments too, to the greatest degree of their rage and cruelty.

1. There is in God a sufficiency of power to keep them that have laid their soul at his foot to be preserved. And hence he is called the soul-keeper, the soul-preserver, (Prov 24:12) "The Lord is thy keeper: the Lord is thy shade upon thy right hand. The sun shall not smite thee by day, nor the moon by night. The Lord shall preserve thee from all evil: he shall preserve thy soul" (Psa 121:5-7). "The sun shall not smite thee": that is, persecution shall not dry and wither thee away to nothing (Matt 13:6,21). But that notwithstanding, thou shalt be kept and preserved, carried through and delivered from all evil. Let him therefore commit the keeping of his soul to him, if he is in a suffering condition, that would have it secured and found safe and sound at last. For,

(1.) Then thine own natural weakness, and timorousness shall not overcome thee.—For it shall not be too hard for God. God can make the most soft spirited man as hard as an adamant, harder than flint, yea harder than the northern steel. "Shall iron break the northern iron and the steel?" (Jer 15:12). The sword of him is [used] in vain that lays at a Christian, when he is in the way of his duty to God: if God has taken to him the charge and care of his soul, he can shoe him with brass, and make his hoofs of iron (Deut 33:25). "He can strengthen the spoiled against the strong, so that the spoiled shall come against the fortress" (Amos 5:8; Eze 13:9).

He can turn thee into another man, and make thee that which thou never wast. Timorous Peter, fearful Peter, he could make as bold as a lion. He that at one time was afraid of a sorry girl, he could make at another to stand boldly before the council (Matt 26; Acts 4:13). There is nothing too hard for God. He can say to them that are of a fearful heart, "Be strong, fear not" (Isa 35:4). He can say, Let the weak say I am strong; by such a word, by which he created the world (Zech 12:8).

(2.) Thine own natural darkness and ignorance shall not cause thee to fall; thy want of wit he can supply.—He can say to the fools, be wise; not only by way of correction, but also by way of instruction too. He "hath chosen the foolish things of the world to confound the wise; - yea, things which are despised, - and things which are not, hath God chosen to bring to nought things that are" (1 Cor 1:27,28). Wisdom and might are his: and when, and where he will work, none can at all withstand him. He can give thee the Spirit of wisdom and revelation in the knowledge of his Son (Eph 1:17). Yea, to do this, is that which he challengeth, as that which is peculiar to himself. "Who hath put wisdom in the inward parts? or who hath given understanding to the heart?" (Job 38:36). And that he will do this that he hath promised, yea, promised to do it to that degree, as to make his, that shall be thus concerned for him, to top, and overtop all men that shall them oppose. I, saith he, "will give you a mouth and wisdom, that all your adversaries shall not be able to gainsay nor resist" (Luke 21:15).

(3.) Thine own doubts and mistrusts about what he will do, and about whither thou shalt go, when thou for him hast suffered awhile, he can resolve, yea, dissolve, crush, and bring to nothing.—He can make fear flee far away: and place heavenly confidence in its room. He can bring invisible and eternal things to the eye of thy soul, and make thee see that in those things in which thine enemies shall see nothing, that thou shalt count worth the loss of ten thousand lives to enjoy. He can pull such things out of his bosom, and can put such things into thy mouth; yea, can make thee choose to be gone, though through the flames, than to stay here and die in silken sheets. Yea, he can himself come near and bring his heaven and glory to thee. The Spirit of glory and of God resteth upon them that are but reproached for the name of Christ (1 Peter 4:14). And what the Spirit of glory is, and what is his resting upon his sufferers, is quite beyond the knowledge of the world, and is but little felt by saints at peace. They be they that are engaged, and that are under the lash of Christ; they are they, I say, that have it and that understand something of it.

When Moses went up the first time into the mount to God, the people reproached him for staying with him so long, saying, "As for this Moses, - we wot not what is become of him" (Exo 32:1). Well, the next time he went up thither, and came down, the Spirit of glory was upon him; his face shone, though he wist it not, to his honour, and their amazement (Exo 34:29-35). Also while Stephen stood before the council to be accused, by suborned men, "All that sat in the council, looking steadfastly on him, saw his face as it had been the face of an angel" (Acts 6:15). Those that honour God, he will honour, yea, will put some of his glory upon them, but they shall be honoured. There is none can tell what God can do. He can make those things that in themselves are most fearful and terrible to behold, the most pleasant, delightful, and desirable things. He can make a jail more beautiful than a palace; restraint, more sweet by far than liberty. And "the reproach of Christ greater riches than the treasures in Egypt" (Heb 11:26). It is said of Christ, That "for the joy that was set before him, he endured the cross, despising the shame" (Heb 12:2). But,

2. As there is in God a sufficiency of power to uphold, so there is in him also a sufficiency of comfort and goodness to embolden us: I mean communicative comfort and goodness. Variety of, and the terribleness that attends afflictions, call, not only for the beholding of things, but also a laying hold of them by faith and feeling; now this also is with God to the making of HIS to sing in the night. Paul and Silas sang in prison, the apostles went away from the council rejoicing, when they had shamefully beaten them for their preaching in the temple (Acts 5). But whence came this but from an inward feeling by faith of the love of God, and of Christ, which passeth knowledge? Hence he says to those under afflictions, "Fear none of those things which thou shalt suffer" (Rev 2:10). There are things to be suffered, as well as places to suffer in; and there are things to be let into the soul for its emboldening, as well as things to be showed to it (Rom 5:5).

Now the things to be suffered are many, some of which are thus counted up: "They were tortured, - had cruel mockings and scourgings; - they were stoned, were sawn asunder, were slain with the sword, - were tempted; - they wandered about in sheep-skins, and goat-skins, being destitute, afflicted, tormented" (Heb 11:35-37). These are some of the things that good men of old have suffered for their profession of the name of Jesus Christ. All which they were enabled by him to bear, to bear with patience; to bear with rejoicing; "knowing in themselves that they had in heaven a better, and an enduring substance" (Heb 10:32-34). And it is upon this account that Paul doth call to mind the most dreadful of his afflictions, which he suffered for the gospel sake with rejoicing; and that he tells us that he was most glad, when he was in such infirmities. Yea, it is upon this account that he boasteth, and vaunteth it over death, life, angels, principalities, powers, things present, things to come, height, depth, and every other creature: for he knew that there was enough in that love of God, which was set on him through Christ, to preserve him, and to carry him through all (2 Cor 12:9,10; Rom 8:37-39). That God has done thus, a thousand instances might be given; and that God will still do thus, for that we have his faithful promise (Isa 43:2; 1 Cor 10:13).

To the adversaries of the church these things have also sometimes been shewed, to their amazement and confusion. God shewed to the king of Babylon that he was with the three children in the fiery furnace (Dan 3:24). God shewed to the king of Babylon again, that he would be where HIS were, though in the lion's den (6:24).

Also, in later days, whoso reads Mr. Fox's Acts and Monuments, will also find several things to confirm this for truth. God has power over all plagues, and therefore can either heighten, or moderate and lessen them at pleasure. He has power over fire, and can take away the intolerable heat thereof. This those in the Marian days could also testify, namely, Hauks and Bainham, and others, who could shout for joy, and clap their hands in the very flames for joy. God has power over hunger, and can moderate it, and cause that one meal's meat shall go as far as forty were wont to do. This is witness in Elias, when he went for his life to the mount of God, being fled from the face of Jezebel (1 Kings 19:8). And what a good night's lodging had Jacob when he fled from the face of his brother Esau: when the earth was his couch, the stone his pillow, the heavens his canopy, and the shades of the night his curtains (Gen 27:12-16).

I can do all things, said Paul, through Christ strengthening me. And again, I take pleasure in infirmities, in reproaches, in necessities, in persecutions, in distresses for Christ's sake. But how can that be, since no affliction for the present seems joyous? I answer, though they be not so in themselves, yet Christ, by his presence, can make them so: for then his power rests upon us. When I am weak, saith he, then I am strong; then Christ doth in me mighty things: for my strength, saith Christ, is made perfect in weakness; in affliction, for the gospel sake.

For when my people are afflicted and suffer great distress for me, then they have my comforting, supporting, emboldening, and upholding presence to relieve them: an instance of which you have in the three children and in Daniel, made mention of before. But what, think you, did these servants of the God of Jacob feel, feel in their souls, of his power and comforting presence when they, for his name, were suffering of the rage of their enemies,—while, also, one, like the Son of God, was walking in the fire with the three; and while Daniel sat and saw that the hands of the angels were made muzzles for the lions' mouths.

I say, was it not worth being in the furnace and in the den to see such things as these? O! the grace of God, and his Spirit and power that is with them that suffer for him, if their hearts be upright with him; if they are willing to be faithful to him; if they have learned to say, here am I, whenever he calls them, and whatever he calls them to. "Wherefore," when Peter saith, "let them that suffer according to the will of God, commit the keeping of their souls to him in well-doing, as unto a faithful Creator." He concludes, that how outrageous, furious, merciless, or cruel soever the enemy is, yet there, with him, they shall find help and succour, relief and comfort; for God is able to make such as do so, stand.

Conclusion Eighth. We will now come to touch upon that which may more immediately be called the reason of this exhortation; for, although all these things that have been mentioned before may, or might be called reasons of the point, yet there are those, in my judgment, that may be called reasons, which are yet behind. As,

1. Because, when a man has, by faith and prayer, committed the keeping of his soul to God, he has the advantage of that liberty of soul to do and suffer for God that he cannot otherwise have. He that has committed his soul to God to keep is rid of that care, and is delivered from the fear of its perishing for ever. When the Jews went to stone Stephen they laid their clothes down at a distance from the place, at a young man's feet, whose name was Saul, that they might not be a cumber or a trouble to them, as to their intended work. So we, when we go about to drive sin out of the world, in a way of suffering for God's truth against it, we should lay down our souls at the feet of God to care for, that we may not be cumbered with the care of them ourselves; also, that

our care of God's truth may not be weakened by such sudden and strong doubts as will cause us faintingly to say, But what will become of my soul? When Paul had told his son Timothy that he had been before that lion Nero, and that he was at present delivered out of his mouth, he adds, And the Lord shall deliver me from every evil work, and will preserve me unto his heavenly kingdom. He shall and will. Here is a man at liberty, here are no cumbersome fears. But how came the apostle by this confidence of his well-being and of his share in another world? Why, "he had committed the keeping of his soul to God," compare 2 Timothy 1:12 with 4:18. For to commit the keeping of the soul to God, if it be done in faith and prayer, it leaves, or rather brings this holy boldness and confidence into the soul.

Suppose a man in the country were necessitated to go to London, and had a great charge of money to pay in there; suppose, also, that the way thither was become exceeding dangerous because of the highwaymen that continually abide therein,—what now must this man do to go on his journey cheerfully? Why, let him pay in his money to such an one in the country as will be sure to return it for him at London safely. Why, this is the case, thou art bound for heaven, but the way thither is dangerous. It is beset everywhere with evil angels, who would rob thee of thy soul, What now? Why, if thou wouldest go cheerfully on in thy dangerous journey, commit thy treasure, thy soul, to God to keep; and then thou mayest say, with comfort, Well, that care is over: for whatever I meet with in my way thither, my soul is safe enough: the thieves, if they meet me, can not come at that; I know to whom I have committed my soul, and I am persuaded that he will keep that to my joy and everlasting comfort against the great day.

This, therefore, is one reason why we should, that suffer for Christ, commit the keeping of our souls to God; because a doubt about the well-being of that will be a clog, a burden, and an affliction to our spirit: yea, the greatest of afflictions, whilst we are taking up our cross and bearing it after Christ. The joy of the Lord is our strength, and the fear of perishing is that which will be weakening to us in the way.

2. We should commit the keeping of our souls to God, because the final conclusion that merciless men do sometimes make with the servants of God is all on a sudden. They give no warning before they strike. We shall not need here to call you to mind about the massacres that were in Ireland, Paris, Piedmont, and other places, where the godly, in the night before they were well awake, had, some of them, their heart blood running on the ground. The savage monsters crying out, Kill, kill, from one end of a street or a place to the other. This was sudden; and he that had not committed his soul to God to keep it was surely very hard put to it now; but he that had done so was ready for such sudden work. Sometimes, indeed, the axe, and halter, or the faggot is shewed first; but sometimes, again, it is without that warning. Up, said Saul to Doeg, the Edomite, and slay the priests of the Lord (1 Sam 22:11,18,19). Here was sudden work: fall on, said Saul, and Doeg fell upon them, "and slew on that day four score and five persons that did wear a linen ephod." "Nob, also, the city of the priests, smote he with the edge of the sword,

both men and women, children and sucklings," &c. Here was but a word and a blow. Thinkest thou not, who readest these lines, that all of these who had before committed their soul to God to keep were the fittest folk to die?

"And immediately the king sent an executioner, and commanded his head to be brought" (Mark 6:27). The story is concerning Herod and John the Baptist: Herod's dancing girl had begged John the Baptist's head, and nothing but his head must serve her turn; well, girl, thou shalt have it. Have it? Ay, but it will be long first. No; thou shalt have it now, just now, immediately. "And immediately he sent an executioner, and commanded his head to be brought."

Here is sudden work for sufferers: here is no intimation beforehand. The executioner comes to John; now, whether he was at dinner, or asleep, or whatever he was about, the bloody man bolts in upon him, and the first word he salutes him with is, Sir, strip, lay down your neck, for I am come to take away your head. But hold, stay; wherefore? pray, let me commit my soul to God. No, I must not stay; I am in haste: slap, says his sword, and off falls the good man's head. This is sudden work; work that stays for no man; work that must be done by and by; immediately, or it is not worth a rush. I will, said she, that thou give me, by and by, in a charger, the head of John the Baptist. Yea, she came in haste, and hastily the commandment went forth, and immediately his head was brought.

3. Unless a man commits the keeping of his soul to God, it is a question whether he can hold out and stand his ground, and wrestle with all temptations. "This is the victory, - even our faith"; and "who is he that overcometh the world, but he that believeth?" And what encouragement has a man to suffer for Christ, whose heart cannot believe, and whose soul he cannot commit to God to keep it? And our Lord Jesus intimates as much when he saith, "Be thou faithful unto death and I will give thee a crown of life." Wherefore saith he thus? but to encourage those that suffer for his truth in the world, to commit the keeping of their souls to him, and to believe that he hath taken the charge and care of them. Paul's wisdom was, that he was ready to die before his enemies were ready to kill him. "I am now ready," saith he, "to be offered and the time of my departure is at hand" (2 Tim 4:6).

This is, therefore, a thing of high concern; to wit, the committing of the soul to God to keep it. It is, I say, of concern to do it now, just now, quickly, whether thou art yet engaged or no; for it is a good preparatory to, as well as profitable in, a time of persecution: consider it, I say. The apostle Paul saith that he and his companions were bold in their God, to profess and stand to the word of God (1 Thess 2:2). But how could that be if they had the salvation of their souls to seek, and that to be sure they would have had, had they not committed the keeping of their souls to him in well-doing?

Quest. But what is committing of the soul to God?

Answ. I have, in general, briefly spoken to that already, and now, for thy further help, we will a little enlarge. Wherefore,

(1.) To commit is to deliver up to custody to be kept. Hence prisoners, when sent to the jail, are said to be committed thither. Thus Paul, "haling men and women, committing them to prison" (Acts 8:3). And thus Joseph's master committed all his prisoners to him, to his custody, to be kept there according to the law (Gen 39:22).

(2.) To commit, is not only to deliver up to custody, but to give in charge; that that which is committed be kept safe, and not suffered to be lost (Luke 16:11). Thus Paul was committed to prison, the jailor being charged to keep him safely (Acts 16:23).

(3.) To commit, is to leave the whole disposal, sometimes, of that which is committed to those to whom such thing is committed. Thus were the shields of the temple committed to the guard (1 Kings 14:27) And Jeremiah to the hands of Gedaliah (Jer 39:14).

And thus thou must commit thy soul to God and to his care and keeping. It must be delivered up to his care and put under his custody. Thou mayest also, though I would speak modestly, give him a charge to take the care of it. "Concerning my sons [and concerning my daughters] and concerning the work of my hands, command ye me" (Isa 45:11). Thou must also leave all the concerns of thy soul and of thy being an inheritor of the next world wholly to the care of God. He that doth this in the way that God has bid him is safe, though the sky should fall. "The poor committeth himself unto thee, thou art the helper of the fatherless" (Psa 10:14).

And for encouragement to do this, the Lord has bidden us, the Lord has commanded us, the Lord expecteth that we should thus do. Yea, thou art also bidden to commit thy way unto him (Psa 37:5). Thy work unto him (Prov 16:3). Thy cause unto him (Job 5:8). Thy soul to him, and he will take care of all. And if we do this, as we should, God will not only take care of us and of our souls in the general, but that our work and ways be so ordered that we may not fail in either. "I have trusted," said David, "in the Lord, therefore I shall not slide" (Psa 26:1).

Before I leave this, I will speak something of the way in which this commitment of the soul to God must be; and that is, "in a way of well-doing." Let them commit the keeping of their souls to him "in well-doing"; or, in a way of well-doing. That is, therefore, the course that a godly man should be found in, at, in, and after he hath committed his soul to God to keep. And, as the apostle says in another place, this is but a "reasonable service" (Rom 12:1). For if God be so gracious as to take care of my soul at my request, why should not I also be so gracious as to be found in a way of well-doing at his bidding? Take care, master, of me for meat and wages, and I will take care, master, that thy work shall be faithfully done. This is honest, and thus should

Christians say to God: and he that heartily, in this, shall mean as he saith, shall find that God's ways shall be strength unto him.

A Christian is not to commit his soul unto God to keep, and so to grow remiss, carnal, negligent, cold, and worldly; concluding as if he had now bound God to save him, but sets himself at liberty whether he will longer serve him in trying and troublesome times or no. He must commit the keeping of his soul to him "in well-doing." He may not now relinquish God's cause, play the apostate, cast off the cross, and look for heaven notwithstanding. He that doth thus will find himself mistaken, and be made to know at last that God takes the care of no such souls. "If any man draws back," saith he, "my soul shall have no pleasure in him." Wherefore, he that committeth the keeping of his soul to God must do it in that way which God has prescribed to him, which is in a way of well-doing. Alas! alas! there is never such a word in it, it must be done in a way of "well-doing." You must think of this that would commit your souls to God in suffering and troublesome times. You must do it in well-doing.

"In well-doing," that is, in persevering in ways of godliness, both with respect to morals and also instituted worship. Thou, therefore, that wouldest have God take care of thy soul, as thou believest, so thou must do well; that is, do good to the poor, to thy neighbour, to all men, especially to the household of faith. Benjamin must have a Benjamin's mess; and all others, as thou art capable, must feel and find the fruit of thy godliness. Thou must thus serve the Lord with much humility of mind, though through many difficulties and much temptation.

Thou must also keep close to gospel worship, public and private; doing of those things that thou hast warrant for from the word, and leaving of that or those things for others that will stick to them—that have no stamp of God upon them. Thou must be found doing of all with all thy heart, and if thou sufferest for so doing, thou must bear it patiently. For what Peter saith to the women he spake to, may be applied to all believers, "whose daughters ye are," saith he, meaning Sarah's, "as long as ye do well, and are not afraid with any amazement" (1 Peter 3:6).

So then, the man that has committed his soul to God to keep has not at all disengaged himself from his duty, or took himself off from a perseverance in that good work that, under a suffering condition, he was bound to do before. No; his very committing of his soul to God to keep it has laid an engagement upon him to abide to God in that calling wherein he is called of God. To commit my soul to God, supposes my sensibleness of hazard and danger; but there is none [no danger] among men when the offence of the cross is ceased. To commit my soul to God to keep, concludes my resolution to go on in that good way of God that is so dangerous to my soul, if God taketh not the charge and care thereof. For he that saith in his heart, I will now commit my soul to God, if he knows what he says, says thus: I am for holding on in a way of bearing of my cross after Christ, though I come to the same end for so doing as he came to before me. This is committing the soul to him in well-doing. Look to yourselves, therefore, whoever you are that talk of leaving your souls with God, but do live loose, idle, profane, and wicked lives. God will not take care of such men's souls; they commit them not unto him as they should. They do but flatter him with their lips and lie unto him with their tongue, and think to deceive the Lord; but to no purpose. "He that soweth to the flesh shall of the flesh reap corruption." It is he that sows to the Spirit that shall "reap life everlasting" (Gal 6:7,8).

[SECOND—A DESCRIPTION OF THE PERSONS WHO ARE DIRECTED TO COMMIT THE KEEPING OF THEIR SOULS TO GOD.]

I shall now come to the second thing contained in the text, namely, to give you a more distinct description of the men that are thus bid to commit the keeping of their souls to God. And they are thus described: they that "suffer according to the will of God." "Let them that suffer according to the will of God commit the keeping of their souls to him in well-doing, as unto a faithful Creator."

Two things are here to be inquired into. FIRST, What the apostle here means by the will of God. SECOND, What suffering according to the will of God is.

FIRST, For the will of God, it is divers ways taken in the scriptures; as, sometimes, for electing, justifying, sanctifying acts of God; sometimes for faith, good life, and sometimes for suffering for his name (Rom 9; Eph 1:11; John 7:17; 1 John 3:23; 1 Thess 4:3; Matt 7:21). But, by will of God here we must, First, Understand HIS LAW AND TESTAMENT. Second, HIS ORDER AND DESIGNMENT.

[THE WILL OF GOD MEANS HIS LAW AND TESTAMENT.]

First, By his will I understand his law and testament. This is called the revealed will of God, or that by which he has made himself, and how he will be worshiped, known unto the children of men. Now, I, understanding these words thus, must, before I go further, make this distinction, to wit, that there is a difference to be put betwixt them that suffer for the breach and those that suffer for keeping of this law and testament; for though both of them may suffer by the will of God, yet they are not both concerned in this text. A malefactor that suffereth for his evil deeds the due punishment thereof, suffereth, as other texts declare, according to the will of God. But, I say, this text doth not concern itself with them; for both this text and this epistle is writ for the counsel and comfort of those that suffer for keeping the law and testament of God; that suffer for well- doing (1 Peter 3:13,14,17; 4:13,14).

The man then that is concerned in this advice is he that suffereth from the hands of men for keeping of the word of God; and this is he that has licence, leave, yea, a command to commit the keeping of his soul to God in well-doing, as unto a faithful Creator. We will a little enlarge upon this.

[What it is to suffer according to the will of God, or his law and testament.]

He that keepeth the word of God is such an one that has regard to both the matter and manner thereof. The matter is the truth, the doctrine contained therein; the manner is that comely, godly, humble, faithful way of doing it which becomes a man that has to do with the law and testament of God; and both these are contained in the text. For, first, here is the will of God to be done; and then, secondly, to be done according to his will. "Let them that suffer according to his will": which words, I say, take in both matter and manner of doing. So then, the man that here we have to do with, and to discourse of, is a man that, in the sense now given, suffereth. That which makes a martyr, is suffering for the word of God after a right manner; and that is, when he suffereth, not only for righteousness, but for righteousness' sake; not only for truth, but of love to truth; not only for God's word, but according to it, to wit, in that holy, humble, meek manner as the word of God requireth. A man may give his body to be burned for God's truth, and yet be none of God's martyrs (1 Cor 13:1-3). Yea, a man may suffer with a great deal of patience, and yet be none of God's martyrs (1 Peter 2:20). The one, because he wanteth that grace that should poise his heart, and make him right in the manner of doing; the other, because he wanteth that word of the Holy One that alone can make his cause good, as to matter. It is, therefore, matter and manner that makes the martyr; and it is this man that is intended in the text which is aforesaid described. So then, they that suffer for the law and testament of God in that holy and humble manner that the Word requires, they are they that, by this Word of God, are commanded to commit the keeping of their souls to God.

From this consideration, two things present themselves to our sight. 1. That a man may be a Christian, and suffer, and yet not suffer, in the sense last given, according to the will of God. 2. There have been, and may yet be a people in the world that have, and may suffer in the sense of the apostle here, according to the will of God.

[1. A Christian may suffer, but not in the sense of the apostle, according to the will of God.]

A few words to the first of these, namely, that a man may be a Christian, and suffer, and yet not suffer, in the sense of the apostle in the text, "according to the will of God." He may be a Christian and yet not suffer as a Christian. He may want the matter, or, he may want the manner, of suffering as a Christian.

This is evident from what this apostle suggests in several places of this epistle. For,

Saith he, "If ye be buffeted for your faults" (1 Peter 2:20). This supposeth that a Christian may so be; for he speaketh here to the same people, unto whom he speaketh in the text, though he putteth them not under the same circumstance, as suffering for well-doing. If ye be buffeted for your faults, for what God's word calls faults, what thank have you from God, or good men, though you take it patiently?

So again, "For it is better, if the will of God be so, that ye suffer for well-doing, than for evil-doing" (1 Peter 3:17). Here it is plainly supposed that a Christian man may suffer for evil-doing, yea, that the will of God may be, that he should suffer for evil- doing. For God, if Christians do not well, will vindicate himself by punishing of them for their doing ill. Yea, and will not count them worthy, though they be his own, to be put among the number of those that suffer for doing well.

Again, "But let none of you suffer as a murderer, or as a thief, or as an evildoer, or as a busybody in other men's matters" (1 Peter 4:15). These are cautions to Christians to persuade them to take heed to themselves, their tongues and their actions, that all be kept within the bounds of the Word. For it would be a foolish thing to say, that these are cautions to persuade to take heed of that, into which it is not possible one should fall. It is possible for Christians to suffer for evil-doing, and therefore let Christians beware; it is possible for Christians to be brought to public justice for their faults, and therefore let Christians beware. It is possible for Christians to suffer justly by the hand of the magistrate, and therefore let Christians beware. This also is insinuated in the text itself, and therefore let Christians beware.

The causes of this are many, some of which I shall now briefly touch upon.

(1.) Sin is in the best of men: and as long as it is so, without great watchfulness, and humble walking with God, we may be exposed to shame and suffering for it. What sin is it that a child of God is not liable to commit, excepting that which is the sin unpardonable? Nor have we a promise of being kept from any other sin, but on condition that we do watch and pray (Matt 26:41).

(2.) It is possible for a Christian to have an erroneous conscience in some things, yea, in such things as, if God by his grace prevents not, may bring us to public justice and shame. Abishai, though a good man, would have killed the king, and that of conscience to God, and love to his master (1 Sam 26:7,8). And had David delivered him up to Saul for his attempt, he had in all likelihood died as a traitor. Peter drew his sword, and would have fought therewith, a thing for which he was blamed of his Master, and bid with a threatening, to put it up again (Matt 26:52). Besides, oppression makes a wise man mad; and when a man is mad what evils will he not do? Further, The devil, who is the great enemy of the Christians, can send forth such spirits into the world as shall not only disturb men, but nations, kings, and kingdoms, in raising divisions, distractions and rebellions. And can so manage matters that the looser sort of Christians may be also dipped and concerned therein. In Absalom's conspiracy against his father, there were two hundred men called out of Jerusalem to follow him, "and they went in their simplicity, not knowing any thing" (2 Sam 15:11). I thank God I know of no such men, nor thing: but my judgment tells me, that if Christians may be drawn into fornication, adultery, murder, theft, blasphemy or the like, as they may; why should it be thought impossible for them to be drawn in here. Wherefore I say again, watch and pray, fear God, reverence his Word, approve of his appointments, that you may be delivered from every evil work and way.

I said afore that the will of God may be, that a Christian should suffer as an evil-doer; but then it is because he keepeth not within the bounds of that, which is also called the will of God. The will of God is, that sin should be punished, though committed by the Christians; punished according to the quality of transgressions: and therefore it is that he hath ordained magistrates. Magistrates, to punish sin, though it be the sin of Christians. They are the ministers of God, revengers, to execute wrath, the wrath of God upon them that do evil (Rom 13). Wherefore, though the Christian as a Christian is the only man at liberty, as called thereunto of God; yet his liberty is limited to things that are good: he is not licensed thereby to indulge the flesh. Holiness and liberty are joined together, yea our call to liberty, is a call to holiness. Seek, and you shall find, that a quiet and peaceable life, in our respective places, under the government, is that which we should pray for, to wit, that we may without molestation, if it were "the will of God," spend our days in all godliness and honesty among our neighbours. See 1 Timothy 2:1-8; 1 Peter 2:13-17.

[First. Caution to Christians as Christians.] —I would improve this a little, and first, to Christians as Christians: beware the cautions, that are here presented to you, be not neglected by you. The evils are burning hot, as hot as a red hot iron. It is the greatest blemish that can be to a Christian, to suffer as an evil- doer. To say nothing of the reproach that such do bring to the name of Christ, their Lord; to his law, their rule; and to the Christian profession, which should be their glory: the guilt and shame that evil actions will load the conscience with at such a time, can hardly be stood under. The man that suffereth as an evil-doer, and yet weareth the name of a Christian, what stumbling blocks doth he lay in the way of the ignorant in a kingdom? The devil told them before, that a Christian was a mischievous man; and to suffer for evil-doing, confirms them in that belief.

Consider also the difficulties that surely such must meet with in the last minutes of their life. For can it be imagined but that such an one must have combats and conflicts at the last, who carry in their consciences the guilt and condemnation that is due to their deeds, to the place which magistrates have appointed for them to receive the reward of their works at. Such an one bereaves not only his own soul of peace, and his name of credit, but himself of life, his friends of all cause of rejoicing, and casteth reproach upon religion, as he is stepping out of the world. What shall I say, Christians as Christians have other things to do than to concern themselves in evil things, or to meddle in other men's matters. Let us mind our own business, and leave the magistrate to his work, office and calling among men also.

I speak now to them that are not by the king called to that employ. A Christian as such has enough to do at home, in his heart, in his house, in his shop, and the like. But if thou must needs be meddling, consider what place, office, calling or relation, God has put thee in, and busy thyself by the rule of the Word to a conscientious performance of that. Nor shalt thou want dignity, though thou art but a private Christian. Every Christian man is made a king by Christ (Rev 5:10). But then, his dominion as such, doth reach no further than to himself. He has not dominion over another's faith (2 Cor 1:24). His office is to govern, and bridle, and keep under, himself; to watch over himself, and to bring his body into subjection to the will of God. The weapons that he has for this purpose are not carnal, but spiritual, and mighty through God. Let him govern then, if he will be a governor, his whole man by the Word. Let him bring down, if he must be bringing down, his own high imaginations, and every high thing that exalts itself against the knowledge of God. If he must be a warrior, let him levy war against his own unruly passions, and let him fight against those lusts that war against his soul (2 Cor 10:3-5; Gal 5:17; James 3:3-8; 1 Peter 2:11).

I say therefore, if thou wilt needs be a ruler, thou hast a tongue, rule that; lusts, rule them; affections, govern them; yea, thou hast excellent graces, manage them, cherish, strengthen and replenish them according to the mind of that great one who has bestowed such power to rule, upon thee. Mortify therefore your members which are upon the earth; fornication, uncleanness, inordinate affection, evil concupiscence, and covetousness, which is idolatry (Col 3:5). Nor do I think that murmuring, shrinking, wincing, complaining, and the like, when men, governors, lay a yoke upon our necks, flow from any thing else, but love to our flesh, and distrust of the faithfulness of God to manage men, things, and actions for his church. The powers that be are ordered as well as ordained of God. They are also always in God's hand, as his rod or staff for the good and benefit of his people. Wherefore we ought with all meekness and humbleness of mind to accept of what our God by them shall please to lay upon us (1 Peter 5:6). By what I now say, I do not forbid groaning and crying to God under affliction. I speak against striving to deliver ourselves from the affliction. And since men are, as I said, the rod, staff or sword in God's hand, we should apply ourselves unto him in faith in a way of prayer, intercession, supplication and giving of thanks for governors. For since they are sent of God, they must needs come with some good in their hand for us, also our prayers may make them more profitable to us. And this we ought to do without wrath and doubting; for this is that which is good, and acceptable unto God (1 Tim 2).

Besides, it is a sign that we forget ourselves when we complain for the punishment of our sins. If we look into ourselves, and ways, we shall see cause of more heavy stripes than yet God by men has laid upon us. What sin has yet been suppressed by all that has happened to us: if pride, covetousness, looseness, treacherous dealing, schisms, and other things, redressed by all the affliction that we have had? Yea, do we not grow worse and worse? Wherefore then should we complain? Where is repentance, reformation, and amendment of life amongst us? Why, then, do we shrink and winch. For my part, I have ofttimes stood amazed both at the mercy of God, and the favour of the Prince towards us; and can give thanks to God for both: and do make it my prayer to God for the king, and that God will help me with meekness and patience to bear whatever shall befall me for my professed subjection to Christ, by men.

We are bid, as I said afore, to give thanks to God for all men, for kings, and for all that are in authority. Because, as I said, there is no man with whom we have to do, we doing as we should, but he bringeth some good thing to us, or doth some good thing for us. We will now descend from them that are supreme in authority, and will come to inferior men: and suppose some of them to act beyond measure, cruelly. What? Can no good thing come to us out of this? Do not even such things as are most bitter to the flesh, tend to awaken Christians to faith and prayer, to a sight of the emptiness of this world, and the fadingness of the best it yields? Doth not God by these things ofttimes call our sins to remembrance, and provoke us to amendment of life? how then can we be offended at things by

which we reap so much good, and at things that God makes so profitable for us?
Doth not God, ofttimes, even take occasions by the hardest of things that come upon us, to visit our souls with the comforts of his Spirit, to lead us into the glory of his word, and to cause us to savour that love that he has had for us, even from before the world began, till now. A nest of bees and honey did Samson find, even in the belly of that lion that roared upon him. And is all this no good? or can we be without such holy appointments of God? Let these things be considered by us, and let us learn like Christians to kiss the rod, and love it.

I have thought, again, my brethren, since it is required of us that we give thanks to God for all these men, it follows that we do with quietness submit ourselves under what God shall do to us by them. For it seems a paradox to me, to give thanks to God for them, that yet I am not willing should abide in that place that God has set them in for me. I will then love them, bless them, pray for them, and do them good. I speak now of the men that hurt me as was hinted afore. And I will do thus, because it is good so to do, because they do me good by hurting of me, because I am called to inherit a blessing, and because I would be like my heavenly Father. "Therefore if mine enemy hunger, let me feed him; if he thirst, let me give him drink" (Matt 5:43-48; 1 Peter 3:9; Rom 12:17-20). (1.) We must see good in that, in which other men can see none. (2.) We must pass by those injuries that other men would revenge. (3.) We must shew we have grace, and that we are made to bear what other men are not acquainted with. (4.) Many of our graces are kept alive by those very things that are the death of other men's souls.

Where can the excellency of our patience, of our meekness, of our long-suffering, of our love, and of our faith appear, if it be not under trials, and in those things that run cross to our flesh? The devil, they say, is good when he is pleased. But Christ and his saints, when displeased.

Let us therefore covet to imitate Christ and the scripture saints. Let us shew out of a good conversation, our works with meekness of wisdom. Let us take heed of admitting the least thought in our minds of evil, against God, the king, or them that are under him in employ, because, the cup, the king, all men, and things are in the hand of God (Psa 75:8; Prov 8:15; 21:1; Lam 3:37). And he can make them better to us, than if they were as our flesh desireth they should.

I have often thought that the best Christians are found in the worst of times: and I have thought again, that one reason why we are no better, is because God purges us no more (John 15). I know these things are against the grain of the flesh, but they are not against the graces of the Spirit. Noah and Lot, who so holy as they, in the day of their affliction? Noah and Lot, who so idle as they in the day of their prosperity? I might have put in David too, who, while he was afflicted, had ways of serving God that were special; but when he was more enlarged, he had ways that were not so good. Wherefore the first ways of David are the ways that God has commended: but the rest of his ways, such as had not pre-eminence (2 Chron 17:3).

We have need of all, and of more than all that has yet befallen us: and are to thank God, since his word and patience have done no more good to us, that he hath appointed men to make us better. Wherefore for a conclusion, as we are to receive with meekness the engrafted word of God, so also we are with patience to bear what God, by man, shall lay upon us. O that saying of God to them of old, "Why criest thou for thine affliction? thy sorrow is incurable for the multitude of thine iniquity: because thy sins were increased, I have done these things unto thee" (Jer 30:15). We have need to consider of, and to sit still and be quiet, and reverence the ordinance of God: I mean affliction. And until we can in truth get hither in our spirits, I neither look to find very right Christianity amongst us, nor much of God among professors. When I think of Mordecai, and Daniel, yea, and of David too, and of the behaviour of them all with respect to the powers that they were under, I cannot but think that a sweet, meek, quiet, loving, godly submission unto men for the Lord's sake, is an excellent token of the grace of God in us. But,

[Second Caution to Weak Christians.] —As I cannot but condemn the actions of such Christians as have been touched before, so I would caution weak Christians not to be offended with true religion for the miscarriages of their fellows. There are two things that are very apt to be an occasion of offence to the weak: one is, when the cross attends religion; the other is, when others that profess religion do suffer for evil-doing. To both these I would say this:—

1. Though the cross, indeed, is grievous to the flesh, yet we should with grace bear up under it, and not be offended at it.

2. And as to the second, though we should and ought to be offended with such miscarriage; yet not with religion, because of such miscarriage. Some, indeed, when they see these things, take offence against religion itself; yea, perhaps, are glad of the occasion, and so fall out with Jesus Christ, saying to him, because of the evils that attend his ways, as the ten tribes said to

Rehoboam, the son of Solomon the king, "What portion have we in David? neither have we inheritance in the son of Jesse; to your tents, O Israel: now see to thine own house, David," (1 Kings 12:16); and so go quite away from him, and cleave no more unto him, to his people, or to his ways: but this is bad. Shun, therefore, the evil ways of Christians, but cleave to the way that is Christian: cast away that bad spirit that thou seest in any, but hold fast to thy Head and Lord. Whither canst thou go? the Lord Jesus has the words of eternal life (John 6:68). Whither wilt thou go? there is not salvation in any other (Acts 4:12). Take heed, therefore, of picking a quarrel with Jesus Christ, and with his ways, because of the evil-doings of some of his followers. Judas sold him, Peter denied him, and many of his disciples went back and did walk no more with him; but neither himself nor his ways were the worse for that. Beware, therefore, that thou truly distinguish between the good ways of Jesus Christ and the evil ways of them that profess him: and take not an occasion to throw away thy own soul down the throat of hell, because others have vilely cast away their lives by transgressing of the law of God. Nay, let other men's faults make thee more wary; let other men's falls make thee look better to thy goings: shun the rock that he that went before thee did split his ship against; and cry to God to lead thee in a path that is plain and good, because of thy observers.

Further, Let not opposite Christians rejoice when they see that evil hath taken their brother by the heel. Hate the garment, the thing that is bad, and by which the name, and fame, and life of thy brother is so vilely cast away, thou shouldest; and take good heed lest it also touch thee, but yet thou shouldest pity thy brother, mourn for his hard hap, and grieve that a thing so much unbecoming Christianity should be suffered to show the least part of itself among any of those that profess the gospel.

Directions for the shunning of suffering for evil-doing, are they that come next to hand.

Direction 1. Therefore, wouldest thou not suffer as an evil-doer, then take heed of committing of evil. Evil courses bring to evil ends; shun all appearance of evil, and ever follow that which is good. And if ye be followers of that which is good, who will harm you (1 Peter 3:13)? Or if there should be such enemies to goodness in the world as to cause thee for that to suffer, thou needest not be ashamed of thy suffering for well-doing, nor can there be a good man, but he will dare to own and stand by thee in it. Yea, thy sufferings for that will make thee happy, so that thou canst by no means be a loser thereby.

Direction 2. Wouldest thou not suffer for evil-doing, then take heed of the occasions of evil. Take heed of tempting company. Beware of men, for they will deliver thee up. There have been men in the world that have sought to make themselves out of the ruins of other men. This did Judas, and some of the Pharisees (Matt 10:17; Luke 20:19,20). Take heed to thy mouth: "A fool's mouth calleth for strokes,—and his lips are the snare of his soul" (Prov 18:7). Take heed of indulging, and hearkening to the ease of the flesh, and of carnal reasonings, for that will put thee upon wicked things.

Direction 3. Wouldest thou not suffer as an evil-doer, then take heed of hearing of any thing spoken that is not according to sound doctrine: thou must withdraw thyself from such in whom thou perceivest not the words of knowledge. Let not talk against governors, against powers, against men in authority be admitted; keep thee far from an evil matter. My son, says Solomon, fear thou the Lord, and the King, and meddle not with those that are given to change.

Direction 4. Wouldest thou not suffer as an evil-doer, addict not thyself to play with evil, to joke and jest, and mock at men in place and power. Gaal mocked at Abimelech, and said, Who is Abimelech that we should serve him? But he paid for his disdainful language at last (Judg 9). I have heard of an innkeeper here in England, whose sign was the crown, and he was a merry man. Now he had a boy, of whom he used to say, when he was jovial among his guests, This boy is heir to the crown, or this boy shall be heir to the crown; and if I mistake not the story, for these words he lost his life. It is bad jesting with great things, with things that are God's ordinance, as kings and governors are. Yea, let them rather have that fear, that honour, that reverence, that worship, that is due to their place, their office, and dignity. How Paul gave honour and respect unto those that were but deputy-kings and heathen magistrates, will greatly appear, if you do but read his trials before them in the book called, The Acts of the Apostles. And what a charge both he and Peter have left behind them to the churches to do so too, may be found to conviction, if we read their epistles.

Direction 5. Wouldest thou not suffer for evil-doing, then take heed of being offended with magistrates, because by their state acts they may cross thy inclinations. It is given to them to bear the sword, and a command is to thee, if thy heart cannot acquiesce with all things with meekness and patience, to suffer. Discontent in the mind sometimes puts discontent into the mouth; and discontent in the mouth doth sometimes also put a halter about the neck. For as a man, by speaking a word in jest may for that be hanged in earnest; so he that speaks in discontent may die for it in sober sadness. Adonijah's discontent put him upon doing that which cost him his life (1 Kings 2:13,23). Great peace have they that love thy law, and nothing shall offend them; for they are subjected to the will and foot of God.

Direction 6. But, above all, get thy conscience possessed yet more with this, that the magistrate is God's ordinance, and is ordered of God as such: that he is the minister of God to thee for good, and that it is thy duty to fear him, and pray for him, to give thanks to God for him, and to be subject to him as both Paul and Peter admonish us; and that not only for wrath, but for conscience sake (Rom 13:5). For all other arguments come short of binding the soul, where this argument is wanting; until we believe that of God we are bound thereto. I speak not these things, as knowing any that are disaffected to the government; for I love to be alone, if not with godly men, in things that are convenient. But because I appear thus in public, and know not into whose hands these lines may come, therefore thus I write. I speak it also to show my loyalty to the king, and my love to my fellow-subjects; and my desire that all Christians should walk in ways of peach and truth.

[2. That Christians may, and have, suffered according to the will of God.]

I come now to the second thing propounded to be spoken to, as to suffering, which is this.—That there have been, and yet may be, a people in the world that have, and may, suffer in the sense of the apostle here, according to the will of God, or for righteousness' sake.

That there have been such a people in the world, I think nobody will deny, because many of the prophets, Christ, and his apostles, thus suffered. Besides, since the Scriptures were written, all nations can witness to this, whose histories tell at large of the patience and goodness of the sufferers, and of the cruelty of those that did destroy them. And that the thing will yet happen, or come to pass again, both Scripture and reason affirm.

First, Scripture. The text tells us, That God hath put enmity betwixt the woman and her seed, and the serpent and his seed (Gen 3:15). This enmity put, is so fixed that none can remove it so, but that it still will remain in the world. These two seeds have always had, and will have, that which is essentially opposite to one another, and they are "the spirit of truth and the spirit of error" (1 John 4:6), sin and righteousness (3:7,8), light and darkness (1 Thess 5:5). Hence "an unjust man is an abomination to the just; and he that is upright in the way is abomination to the wicked" (Prov 29:27). So that unless you could sanctify and regenerate all men, or cause that no more wicked men should any where be in power for ever, you cannot prevent but that sometimes still there must be sufferers for righteousness' sake. "Yea, and all that will live godly in Christ Jesus shall suffer persecution" (2 Tim 3:12).

Second, To prove this by reason is easy. The devil is not yet shut up in the bottomless pit— Antichrist is yet alive. The government in all kingdoms is not yet managed with such light, and goodness of mind, as to let the saints serve God, as he has said, whatever it is in some. And until then there will be in some places, though for my part I cannot predict where, a people that will yet suffer for well-doing, or for righteousness' sake.

In order to a right handling of this matter, I shall divide this head into these two parts—A. Show you what it is to suffer for well-doing, or for righteousness. B. Show you what it is to suffer for righteousness' sake. I put this distinction, because I find that it is one thing to suffer for righteousness, and another to suffer for righteousness' sake.

[A. What it is to suffer for righteousness.]

To begin with the first, namely, to show you what it is to suffer for righteousness. Now that may be done either passively or actively.

1. Passively, as when any suffer for righteousness without their own will, or consent thereto. Thus, the little children at Bethlehem suffered by the hands of bloody Herod, when they died for, or in the room and stead of, Jesus Christ (Matt 2:16). Every one of those children died for righteousness, if Christ is righteousness; for they died upon his account, as being supposed to be he himself. Thus also the children of Israel's little ones, that were murdered with their parents, or otherwise, because of the religion of them that begat and bare them, died for righteousness. The same may be said concerning those of them that suffered in the land of the Chaldeans upon the same account. I might here also bring in those poor infants that in Ireland, Piedmont, Paris, and other places, have had their throats cut, and their brains dashed out against the walls, for none other cause but for the religion of their fathers. Many, many have suffered for righteousness after this manner. Their will, nor consent, has been in the suffering, yet they have suffered for religion, for righteousness. And as this hath been, so it may be again; for if men may yet suffer for righteousness, even so, for ought I know, even in this sense, may their children also.

Now, although this is not the chief matter of my text, yet a few words here may do no harm. The children that thus suffer, though their own will and consent be not in what they undergo, may yet, for all that, be accepted as an offering unto the Lord. Their cause is good; it is for religion and righteousness. Their hearts do not recoil against the cause for which they suffer; and although they are children, God can deal with them as with John the Baptist, cause them in a moment to leap for joy of Christ; or else can save them by his grace, as he saveth other his elect infants, and thus comprehend them, though they cannot apprehend him; yea, why may they not only be saved, but in some sense be called martyrs of Jesus Christ, and those that have suffered for God's cause in the world? God comforted Rachel concerning her children that Herod murdered in the stead, and upon the account of Christ.

He bids her refrain herself from tears, by this promise, that her children should come again from the land of the enemy, from death. And again, said he, Thy children shall come again to their own border; which I think, if it be meant in a gospel sense, must be to the heavenly inheritance. Compare Jeremiah 31:15- 17 with Matthew 2:18.

And methinks this should be mentioned, not only for her and their sakes, but to comfort all those that either have had, or yet may have, their children thus suffer for righteousness. None of these things, as shall be further showed anon, happen without the determinate counsel of God. He has ordered the sufferings of little children as well as that of persons more in years. And it is easy to think that God can as well foresee which of his elect shall suffer by violent hands in their infancy, as which of them shall then die a natural death. He has saints small in age as well as in esteem or otherwise and sometimes the least member of the body suffereth violence, as well as the head or other chief parts. And although I desire not to see these days again, yet methinks it will please me to see those little ones that thus have already suffered for Jesus, to stand in their white robes with the elders of their people, before the throne, to sing unto the Lamb.

2. Actively. But to pass this, and to come to that which is more directly intended to be spoken to, namely, to show you who doth actively suffer for righteousness. And,

(1.) It is he that chooseth by his own will and consent to suffer for it. All suffering that can be called active suffering, must be by the consent of the will; and that is done when a man shall have sin and suffering set before him, and shall choose suffering rather than sin. He chose "rather to suffer affliction with the people of God, than to enjoy the pleasures of sin for a season" (Heb 11:25). And again, They did not accept of deliverance, that is, of base and unworthy terms, "that they might obtain a better resurrection" (verse 35).

Indeed, no man can force a Christian to suffer as a Christian, without his own consent. All Christians are sufferers of will and consent. Hence it is said, they must take up their cross, by which taking up, an act of their will is intended (Matt 10:38; 16:24). So again, "Take my yoke upon you," which also intends an act of the will (11:29). This, therefore, is the first thing that I would present you with. Not that an act of the will is enough to declare a man a sufferer for righteousness, it standing alone; for a man, through the strength of delusion, and the power of an erroneous conscience, may be willing to suffer for the grossest opinions in the world. But I bring it to show that actual suffering for righteousness must also be by the consent of the will—the mind of the man must be in it.

(2.) He that suffereth for righteousness thus, must also have a good cause. A good cause is that which is essential to suffering for righteousness. A good cause, what is that? Why, verily, it is the truth of God, either in the whole of it, as contained in the Scriptures of truth, or in the parts of it, as set before me to believe, or do, by any part of that holy Word. This may be called the matter for which one suffereth; or, as it is called in another place, "the word of righteousness" (Heb 5:13). It may also be called the form of sound doctrine, or the like. Because without this Word, the matter and nature of God's truths cannot be known. Pilate's question, "What is truth?" will still abide a question, to those that have not, or regard not the Word, the rule of righteousness (John 18:38). See then that thy cause be good, thou that wouldest know what it is to suffer for righteousness; step not an hair's breadth without the bounds of the Word of truth; also take heed of misunderstanding, or of wringing out of its place, any thing that is there. Let the words of the upright stand upright, warp them not, to the end they may comply in show with any crooked notion. And to prevent this, take these three words as a guide, in this matter to thee. They show men their sins, and how to close with a Saviour; they enjoin men to be holy and humble; they command men to submit themselves to authority. And whatever is cross to these, comes from ignorance of, or from wresting, the rule of righteousness out of its place.

But more particularly, the word of righteousness—thy cause, within the bounds of which thou must keep, if thou wilt suffer for righteousness, is to be divided into two parts. (1.) It containeth a revelation of moral righteousness. (2.) It containeth a revelation of evangelical righteousness. As for moral righteousness, men seldom suffer; only, for that. Because that is the righteousness of the world, and that, simply as such, that sets itself up in every man's conscience, and has a testimony for itself, even in the light of nature. Besides, there is nothing that maketh head against that; but that which every man is ashamed, by words to plead for, and that is immorality. And this is that which Peter intends when he saith, "And if ye be followers of that which is good, who will harm you?" (1 Peter 3:13). If ye be followers of moral goodness. But if it should so happen, for the case is rare, that any man should make you sufferers because you love God, and do good to your neighbour, happy are ye. Though I do not think that the apostle's conclusion terminates there. But more of these things anon.

For let a man be a good neighbour in morals; let him feed the hungry, clothe the naked, give freely out of his purse to the poor, and do that which he would another should do to him; and stop there, and not meddle with the name of Christ, and he shall have but few enemies in the world. For it is not the law, but Christ, that is the stumbling-block, and the rock of offence to men (Isa 8:14,15; Rom 9:31-33).

Wherefore, there is in God's Word a revelation of another righteousness—a righteousness which is not so visible to, yea, and that suiteth not so with, the reason of man as that moral righteousness doth. Wherefore this righteousness makes men righteous in principle, and practise so, as is foreign to natural men. Hence it is said to be foolishness to them (1 Cor 2:14). And again, "Its praise is not of men" (Rom 2:29). This righteousness is also revealed in the Scriptures, but the blind cannot see it. It is the work of the Holy Ghost in the heart, and is therefore called the fruits of the Spirit; and the grace, which in the head and fullness of it, is only to be found in Christ (John 1:16; Col 1:19; 1 Tim 1:14). This righteousness being planted in the heart, leads a man out by the Word of God, to seek for another righteousness, as invisible to, and foreign from, the natural man, as this. And that righteousness is that which properly is the righteousness of Jesus Christ—a righteousness that standeth in his obedience to his Father's law, as he was considered a common or public person—a righteousness which he brought into the world, not for himself, as considered in a private capacity, but for those that shall by faith venture themselves upon him, to obtain by him life eternal (Rom 5:19; Phil 3:7-10).

Again, This closing by faith, with this righteousness thus found in Christ, and being taken therewith, leads me yet to another righteousness, which is instituted worship, appointed by Christ, for all his followers to be conversant in; this worship is grounded on positive precepts, and so on words of righteousness, called Christ's words, Christ's sayings, &c.

Now, upon this bottom begins the difference betwixt the men of God and the world. For, first, by this inward principle of righteousness we come to see, and say, that men by nature are not Christians, what privileges soever they may account themselves partakers thereof. But whosoever is a Christian, of God's making so, is begotten and born of God, and made a new creature by the anointing received from the Holy One (James 1:18; John 3:3,5; 2 Cor 5:17,18; 1:21; 1 John 2:20,24,27). Now, this these carnal men cannot endure to hear of; because it quite excludes them, as such, from a share in the kingdom of heaven. To this, again, the Christian stands and backs what he says by the Word of God. Then the game begins, and the men of the world are thoughtful how they may remove such troublesome fellows out of the way. But because the Christians love their neighbours, and will not let them thus easily die in their sins, therefore they contend with them, both by reasonings, writings, sermons, and books of gospel divinity; and stand to what they say. The world, again, are angry with these sayings, sermons, and books, for that by them they are concluded to be persons that are without repentance, and the hope of eternal life. Here again, the carnal world judges that these people are proud, self- willed, pragmatical, contentious, self-conceited, and so unsufferable people. The Christian yet goes on and stands to what he has asserted. Then the poor world at their last shift begins to turn, and overturn the gospel-man's sayings; perverting, forcing, stretching, and dismembering of them; and so making of them speak what was never thought, much less intended by the believer.

Thus they served our Lord; for, not being able to down with his doctrine, they began to pervert his words, and to make, as also they said afterwards of Luther's, some offensive, some erroneous, some treasonable, and that both against God and Caesar, and so they hanged him up, hoping there to put an end to things. But this is but the beginning of things; for the Christian man, by the word of the gospel, goes further with his censure. For he also findeth fault with all that this man, by the ability of nature, can do for the freeing himself from the law of sin and death. He condemns him by the Word, because he is in a state of nature, and he condemneth also whatever, while in that state, he doth, as that which by no means can please God (Rom 14:23; Heb 11:6). This now puts him more out; this is a taking of his gods away from him. This is to strip him of his raiment, such as it is, and to turn him naked into the presence of God. This, I say, puts him out and out. These wild-brained fellows, quote he, are never content, they find fault with us as to our state; they find fault with us as to our works, our best works. They blame us because we are sinners, and they find fault with us, though we mend; they say, by nature we are no Christians, and that our best doings will not make us such. What would they have us do? Thus, therefore, they renew their quarrel; but the Christian man cannot help it, unless he would see them go to hell, and saying nothing. For the Word of God doth as assuredly condemn man's righteousness, as it doth condemn man's sin; it condemneth not man's righteousness among men, for there it is good and profitable (Job 35:6-8), but with God, to save the soul, it is no better than filthy rags (Isa 64:6).

Nor will this Christian man suffer these carnal ones to delude themselves with a change of terms;

for the devil, who is the great manager of carnal men in things that concern their souls, and in the plea that they make for themselves, will help them to tricks and shifts to evade the power of the Word of God. Teaching them to call the beauties of nature grace, and the acts of natural powers the exercise of the graces of the Spirit, he will embolden them also to call man's righteousness the righteousness of Christ, and that by which a sinner may be justified in the sight of God from the law. These tricks the Christian sees, and being faithful to God's truth, and desiring the salvation of his neighbour, he laboureth to discover the fallacy of, and to propound better terms for this poor creature to embrace, and venture his soul upon; which terms are warranted by the New Testament, a stranger to which the natural man is. But, I say, the things which the Christian presseth, being so foreign to nature, and lying so cross to man's best things, are presently judged by the natural man to be fables or foolishness (1 Cor 2:14). Wherefore here again, he takes another occasion to maintain his strife, and contention against the righteous man; raising of slanders upon him, and laying things to his charge that he understandeth not; charging also his doctrine with many grievous things. Namely, that he holdeth that man was made to be damned; that man's righteousness is no better than sin; that a man had as good to do ill as well; that we may believe, and do what we list; that holiness pleaseth not God; and that sinning is the way to cause grace to abound. Besides, say they, he condemneth good motions, and all good beginnings of heart to God-ward; he casteth away that good we have, and would have us depend upon a justice to save us by, that we can by no means approve of. And thus the quarrel is made yet wider between the men of the world and Christian man. But there is not a stop put here.

For it is possible for the carnal man to be beaten out of all his arguments for himself and his own things, by the power and force of the Word; and to be made to consent to what the Christian has said as to the notion of the truth. I must not speak this of all. But yet the breach doth still abide; for that yet there appears to be no more with the man, but only the notion of things. For though the notion of things are those that of God are made the means of conveying of grace into the heart, yet grace is not always with the notion of things; the Word ofttimes standeth in man's understanding alone, and remaineth there, as not being accompanied with such grace as can make it the power of God to salvation. Now, when it is thus with the soul, the danger is as great as ever, because there is a presumption now begotten in the heart that the man is in a saved condition,—a presumption, I say, instead of faith, which puffeth up, instead of enabling the soul after a godly manner to depend upon God for mercy through Christ. This is called the word of them that are puffed up; the word only, because not accompanied with saving grace (1 Cor 4:19; 8:1; 1 Thess 1:5).

This the Christian also sees, and says it is too weak to conduct the soul to glory. And this, indeed, he says, because he would not that his neighbour should come short home. But neither can this be borne; but here again, the natural man with his notion of things is offended; and takes pet against his friend, because he tells him the truth, and would that he so should digest the truth, that it may prove unto him eternal life. Wherefore he now begins to fall out again, for as yet the enmity is not removed; he therefore counts him an unmerciful man, one that condemneth all to hell but himself; and as to his singularity in things, those he counteth for dreams, for enthusiasms, for allegorical whimsies, vain revelations, and the effects of an erroneous judgment. For the Lord has put such darkness betwixt Egypt and Israel, as will not suffer them to come together. But this is not all.

For it is possible for these carnal men to be so much delighted in the notion of things, as to addict themselves to some kind of worship of Christ, whose notions of truth have by them been received. And because their love is yet but carnal, and because the flesh is swelling, and is pleased with pomp and sumptuousness, therefore, to show how great an esteem such have for Christ, whom they are now about to worship, they will first count his testament, though good, a thing defective, and not of fullness sufficient to give, in all particular things, direction how they should, to their own content, perform their glorious doctrine. For here and there, and in another place, cry they, there is something wanting. Here, say they, is nothing said of those places, vestures, gestures, shows, and outward greatness that we think seemly to be found in and with those that worship Jesus. Here wants sumptuous ceremonies, glorious ornaments, new fashioned carriages, all which are necessary to adorn worship withal.

But now here again, the truly godly, as he comes to see the evil of things, maketh his objections, and findeth fault, and counts them unprofitable and vain (Isa 29; Matt 15; Mark 7). But they again, seeing the things they have made are the very excellencies of human invention, and things added as a supplement to make up what, and wherein, as they think, that man that was faithful over his own house as a son was defective. They are resolved to stand upon their points, and not to budge an inch from the things that are so laudable, so necessary, so convenient, and so comely; the things that have been judged good, by so many wise, learned, pious, holy, reverend, and good men. Nay, if this were all, the godly would make a good shift; but their zeal is so great for what they have invented, and their spirits so hot to make others couch and bend thereto, that none must be suffered to their power to live and breathe, that refuseth to conform thereto. This has been proved too true, both in France, Spain, Germany, Italy, and other places; and upon this account it is that persecution has been kept alive so many hundred years in some places against the church of God.

From what has been said as to these things, this I collect as the sum—First, That man by nature is in a state of wrath and condemnation (Eph 2:1-4; John 3:18). Secondly, That the natural man, by all his natural abilities, is not able to recover himself from this his condemned condition (John 6:44; Eph 1:19,20). Thirdly, That a man may have right notions of gospel things, that hath no grace in his heart (1 Cor 13:2,3). Fourthly, That to add human inventions to Christ's institutions, and to make them of the same force and necessity, of the same authority and efficacy, is nought; and not to be subjected to (Isa 29:13; Matt 15:8,9; Mark 7:6,7).

So then, he that saith these things, saith true; for the Scriptures say the same. This, then, is a good cause to suffer for, if men will that I shall suffer for saying so; because it is that which is founded upon the Word of God; and the Word is the ground and foundation of all true doctrine. Let him, then, that believeth what is here discoursed, and that liveth soberly and peaceably in this belief among his neighbours, stand by what he hath received, and rejoice that he hath found the truth. And if any shall afflict or trouble him for holding of these things, they afflict or trouble him for holding to good things; and he suffereth at their hands because his cause is good.

And such an one may with boldness, as to this, make his appeal to the Bible, which is the foundation of his principles, and to God the author of that foundation, if what he holds is not good. He may say, "Lord, I have said, that man by nature is in a state of condemnation, and they make me suffer for that. Lord, I have asserted that man, by all his natural abilities, is not able to recover himself from this his condemned state, and they make me suffer for that. Lord, I have said that a natural man may have right notions of the gospel, and yet be without the saving grace thereof, and they make me suffer for that. Lord, I cannot consent that human inventions and doctrines of men should be joined with thy institution as matters of worship, and imposed upon my conscience as such, and they make me suffer for that. Lord, I own the government, pray for my superiors, live quietly among my neighbours, give to all their dues, feed the hungry, clothe the naked, relieve the afflicted, and show myself, by my faith and life, to be a true Christian man, and yet my neighbours will not let me alone. True, I cannot comply with all that some men would have me comply with; no more did Daniel, no more did Paul; and yet Daniel said, that he had to the king done no hurt (Dan 6:22), and Paul said, 'neither against the law of the Jews, neither against the temple, nor yet against Caesar, have I offended anything at all'" (Acts 25:8).

For he that keeps within the compass of God's Word, hurts no man, gives just offence to no man, though he complieth not with all that are modes and ways of worship in the world. Nor can this appeal be judged injurious, if it be not attended with intercessions against them that hate us. But we will pass this, and come to a second thing.

(3.) As he that suffereth for righteousness must have a good cause, so he that suffereth for righteousness must have a good call.

A man, though his cause be good, ought not by undue ways to run himself into suffering for it; nature teaches the contrary, and so doth the law of God. Suffering for a truth ought to be cautiously took in hand, and as warily performed. I know that there are some men that are more concerned here than some; the preacher of the Word is by God's command made the more obnoxious man, for he must come off with a woe, if he preaches not the gospel (1 Cor 9:16). He, therefore, I say, doth and ought more to expose himself than other Christians are called to do. Yet it behoveth him also to beware, because that Christ has said to him, "Behold, I send you forth as sheep, or lambs, in the midst of wolves: be ye therefore wise as serpents, and harmless as doves" (Matt 10:16; Luke 10:3). A man is not bound by the law of his Lord, to put himself into the mouth of his enemy. Christ withdrew himself; Paul escaped the governor's hands, by being let down in a basket over the wall of the city (2 Cor 11:32,33). And Christ hath said, If they persecute you in one city, flee ye to another. If they will not let me preach here, I will take up my Bible, and be gone. Perhaps this is because I must preach in some other place. A minister can quickly pack up, and carry his religion with him, and offer what he knows of his God to another people (Acts 13:44-47). Nor should a minister strive, I think, with the magistrate for place, or time. But let him hearken to hear what God shall say by such opposition. Perhaps the magistrate must drive thee out of this place, because the soul is in another place that is to be converted, or helped by thy sermon today. We must also in all things, show ourselves to be such as by our profession we would that men should believe we are, to wit, meek, gentle, not strivers, but take our Lord and our brethren the prophets for our examples.

But I will not here presume to give instructions to ministers; but will speak a few words in the general about what I think may be a sufficient call to a man to suffer for righteousness.

First, Every Christian man is bound by God's Word to hold to, or stand by his profession, his profession of faith, and to join to that profession an holy godly life; because the Apostle and High priest of his profession is no less a one than Christ Jesus (Heb 3:1; 10:23). This by Christ himself is expressed thus, Let your light so shine (Matt 5:16). No man lighteth a candle to put it under a bushel. Let your loins be girded about, and your lights burning (Luke 12:35). And Paul bids the Philippians hold forth the word of life (Phil 2:16).

And more particularly, by all this, this is intended, that we should hide our faith in Christ from no man, but should rather make a discover of it by a life that will do so; for our profession, thus managed, is the badge, and the Lord's livery, by which we are distinguished from other men. So then, if, while I profess the truth of Christ, and so walk as to make my profession of it more apparent, I be made a sufferer for it, my call is good, and I may be bold in God and in my profession. This, Peter intends when he saith, "But and if ye suffer for righteousness" sake, happy are ye, and be not afraid of their terror, neither be troubled; but sanctify the Lord God in your hearts, and be ready always to give an answer to every man that asketh you a reason of the hope that is in you, with meekness and fear (1 Peter 3:14,15). Here, then, is a call not to meddle with the other, but to mind our own business; to walk in our Christian profession, and to adorn it with all good works; and if any man will meddle with me, and ask me a reason of the hope that I have, to give it him with meekness and fear, whatever follows thereupon. This, Peter should have done himself there, where he denies his Master thrice.

The reason is, for that Christianity is so harmless a thing, that, be it never so openly professed, it hurts no man. I believe that Christ will save me; what hurt is this to my neighbour? I love Christ because he will save me; what hurt is this to any? I will for this worship Christ as he has bid me;

what hurt is this to anybody? I will also tell my neighbours what a loving one my Christ is, and that he is willing to be good to them as he has been good to me; and what hurt is this to the governor of a kingdom? But and if any man will afflict me for this, my cause is good, and also my call to stand full godly to my profession.

Secondly, There is sometimes a call to suffer for righteousness, even from the voice of necessity. That is, either when, by my silence, the truth must fall to the ground; or when, by my shrinking, the souls of other men are in danger. This, I say, is a call to suffer even by the voice of necessity. The case may be when God's ways may be trodden under foot; yea, his Word, and ways, and name, and people, and all. Thus Goliath did do, for several days together (1 Sam 17), and vaunted in his doing; and there was not a man, no, not in Israel, that durst answer him a word. And now was the spirit of David stirred in him, and he would put his life in his hand, and give this man an answer; and he saw there was reason for it—necessity gave him a call. Is there not a cause, saith he, lies bleeding upon the ground, and no man of heart or spirit to put a check to the bold blasphemer? I will go fight with him; I will put my life in my hand; if I die, I die.

Consider also what Daniel did when the law was gone out to forbid, for thirty days, petitioning any god or man, save the king only. At that time, also, not a man of Israel peeped (Dan 6:7). Now necessity walks about the streets, crying, Who is on the Lord's side? Who, &c. And Daniel answers, I am, by opening of his window, and praying, as at other times, three times a day, with his face towards Jerusalem (verse 10). He heard this voice of necessity, and put his life in his hand, and complied with it, to the hazard of being torn in pieces by the lions.

Much like this was that of the three children; for when that golden image was set up, and worship commanded to be done unto it, not one, that we read of, durst stand upright when the time was come that bowing was the sign of worship. Only the three children would not bow: it was necessary that some should show that there was a God in heaven, and that divine worship was due alone to him (Dan 3:10-12). But they run the hazard of being turned to ashes, in a burning fiery furnace, for so doing. But necessity has a loud voice, and shrill in the ears of a tender conscience: this voice will awake jealousy and kindle a burning fire within, for the name, and cause, and way, and people, of the God of heaven.

Thirdly, There is sometimes a call to suffer for righteousness by the voice of providence. That is, when, by providence, I am cast for my profession into the hands of the enemies of God and his truth; then I am called to suffer for it what God shall please to let them lay upon me. Only, for the making of my way more clear in this matter, I will deliver what I have to say, with a caution or two. 1. Thou must take heed that thy call be good to this or that place, at which, by providence, thou art delivered up. 2. Thou must also take heed that, when thou art there, thou busiest thyself in nothing but that that good is. 3. Thou must also take heed that thou stay there no longer than while thou mayest do good or receive good there. 4. Thus far a man is in the way of his duty, and therefore may conclude that the providence of God, under which now he is, is such as has mercy and salvation in the bowels of it, whatsoever is by it, at the present, brought upon him.

Christ Jesus, our Lord, though his death was determined, and of absolute necessity, and that chiefly for which he came into the world, chose rather to be taken in the way of his duty than in any other way or anywhere else. Wherefore, when the hour was come, he takes with him some of his disciples, and goeth into a garden, a solitary place, to pray; which done, he sets his disciples to watch, and falleth himself to prayer. So he prays once; he prays twice; he prays thrice: and he giveth also good doctrine to his disciples. And now, behold, while he was here, in the way of his duty, busying himself in praying to God, and in giving of good instruction to his followers, upon him comes Judas and a multitude with swords and staves, and weapons, to take him; to which providence he, in all meekness, submits, for he knew that by it he had a call to suffer (Matt 26:36-47).

In this way, also, the apostles were called to suffer, even while they were in the way of their duty. Yea, God bid them go into the temple to preach, and there delivered them into the hands of their enemies (Acts 4:1-3; 5:20-26).

Be we in the way of our duty, in the place and about the work unto which we are called of God, whether that work be religious or civil, we may, without fear, leave the issue of things to God, who only doth wonderful things. And he who lets not a sparrow fall to the ground without his providence, will not suffer a hair of our head to perish but by his order (Luke 12:6,7). And since he has engaged us in his work, as he has if he has called us to it, we may expect that he will manage, and also bear us out therein; either so as by giving of us a good deliverance by way of restoration to our former liberty and service for him, or so as to carry us well out of this world to them that, under the altar, are crying, How long, holy and true: nor shall we, when we come there, repent that we suffered for him here. Oh! how little do saints, in a suffering condition, think of the robes, the crowns, the harps, and the Son that shall be given to them; and that they shall have when they come upon mount Zion (Rev 6:11; 14:1-7).

Fourthly, There is sometimes a call to suffer for righteousness by an immediate and powerful impulse of the Spirit of God upon the heart. This, I say, is sometimes, and but sometimes; for this is not God's ordinary way, nor are many of his servants called after this manner to suffer for righteousness. Moses was called thus to suffer when he went so often unto Pharaoh with the message of God in his mouth. And "he endured, as seeing him who is invisible" (Heb 11:25-27).

Paul was called thus to suffer, and he obeyed, and went, and performed that work, according to the will of God. This kind of call Paul calls a binding, or a being bound in the Spirit, because the Holy Ghost had laid such a command upon him to do so, that he could not, by any means, get from under the power of it. "And now, behold," saith he, "I go bound in the Spirit unto Jerusalem, not knowing the things that shall befal me there" (Acts 20:22). For he that is under this call has, as I said, bonds laid upon his spirit, which carry him to the place where his testimony is to be borne for God; nor shall he, if he willingly submits and goes, as Paul did, but have an extraordinary presence of God with him, as he. And see what a presence he had; for after the second assault was given him by the enemy, even "the night following, the Lord stood by him, and said, Be of good cheer, Paul; for as thou hast testified of me in Jerusalem, so must thou bear witness also at Rome" (Acts 23:11). Thus God meeteth his people in their service for him, when he calls them aloud to do great service for him. The power of such a call as this, I say, is great, and men of ordinary spirits must needs give place thereto, and leave a man thus bound to the God that thus has bound him. All the help such can afford him is to follow him with our prayers, not to judge him or grieve him, or lay stumbling-blocks before him. No; they must not weep nor mourn for him, so as to make him sorrowful (Acts 21:12-14).

His friends may suggest unto him what is like to attend his present errand, as Agabus did by the Spirit to Paul when he took his girdle and bound himself therewith, to show him how his enemies should serve him whither he went. "Thus said the Holy Ghost," said he, "so shall the Jews at Jerusalem bind the man that owneth this girdle, and shall deliver him into the hands of the Gentiles" (Acts 21). But if this call be indeed upon a man, all sorrow is turned into joy before him; for he is ready, not only to be bound, but also to die at Jerusalem for the name of the Lord Jesus (Acts 21:13).

Instances, also, of later times might be given of a call extraordinary to suffer for righteousness. For many, in the first three hundred years' persecution, when nobody knew what they were, would boldly come up to the face of their enemies and tell what they were, and suffer for what they professed, the death. I remember, also, the woman who, when her friends were gone before to suffer, how she came running and panting after, for fear she should not come thither time enough to suffer for Jesus Christ.
But I will give you an instance of later times, even in the beginning of Queen Elizabeth's reign, of an Hertfordshire man that went as far as Rome to bear his testimony for God against the wickedness of that place. This man, when he was arrived there, and had told them wherefore he was come, they took and condemned him to death, to wit, to be burned for an heretic. Now he was to ride from the prison to the place of execution upon an ass, with his face to the beast's tail, and was to be stripped from the shoulders to the waist, that he might be tormented all the way he went with burning torches continually thrust to his sides; but he, nothing at all afraid, spake in his exhortation to the people to fly from their sin and idolatry; he would also catch hold of the torches and put them to his sides, to show how little he esteemed the worst that they could do. Also, when he was come to the place of execution, he suffered there such cruelty, with so unconcerned a mind, and with such burning zeal for God's truth, testified against them while he could speak; that, all amazed, his enemies cried, he could not have suffered as he did but by the

help of the devil. His name I have now forgot, but you will find it, with the story at large, in the third volume of Acts and Monuments, at the 1022 page. But we will pass this, and come to our second particular, namely,

[B. What it is to suffer for righteousness' sake.]

To show when it may be said a man doth not only suffer for righteousness, but also for righteousness' sake.

To suffer for righteousness' sake must be either with the intention of the persecutor or else of the persecuted. The persecutor, whatever the person's suffering is, if he afflicteth this person for a supposed good that he thinketh he hath or professeth, he make him suffer for righteousness' sake. So that, in this sense, a man that hath no grace may not only suffer for righteousness, but also for righteousness' sake. But this I intend not, because the text is not concerned with it.

The thing, therefore, now intended to be spoken to, is this, namely, when a man may be said to suffer what he suffereth upon a religious account, of love to, or for the sake of, that good that he finds in the truths of God, or because his heart is joined and espoused to the good of the truths that he professeth; not that there is any thing in any truth of God that is not good; but a man may profess truth, not for the sake of the goodness that is in it, but upon a remote account. Judas professed truth, not of love to the truth, but of love to the bag, and to the money that was put therein. Men may profess for a wife, for a trade, for friendship, or because profession is at such a time or in such a place, in fashion. I wish that there were no cause to say this. Now there is not any of these that profess the truth for the truth's sake, that profess the truth of love to it; nor shall they, should they suffer as professors, never so long, never so much, never so grievously, be counted of God among them that suffer for righteousness' sake; that is, of unfeigned love to righteousness. Wherefore, that I may show you who may be said to suffer for righteousness' sake, I will propound and speak to several things.

1. Then, he that suffereth in the apostle's sense, for well-doing, or for righteousness' sake, sets his face against nothing but sin. He resisteth unto blood, striving against sin. Sin is the object of his indignation, because it is an enemy to God, and to his righteous cause in the world (Heb 12:3,4). Sin, I say, is that which such a man singleth out as his opposite, as his antagonist, and that against which his heart is set. It is a rare thing to suffer aright, and to have my spirit, in my suffering, bent only against God's enemy—sin; sin in doctrine, sin in worship, sin in life, sin in conversation. Now then, he that suffereth for righteousness' sake has singled out sin to pursue it to death, long before he comes to the cross. It is sin, alas, and his hatred to it that have brought him into this condition. He fell out with sin at home, in his own house, in his own heart, before he fell out with sin in the world, or with sin in public worship. For he that can let sin go free and uncontrolled at home within, let him suffer while he will, he shall not suffer for righteousness'

sake. And the reason is, because a righteous soul, as the phrase is, 2 Peter 2:8, has the greatest antipathy against that sin that is most ready to defile it, and that is, as David calls it, one's own iniquity, or the sin that dwelleth in one's own flesh. I have kept me, says he, from mine iniquity, from mine own sin. People that are afraid of fire are concerned most with that that burneth in their own chimney; they have the most watchful eye against that that is like to burn down their own house first.

He also that suffereth for righteousness' sake, doth it also because he would not that sin should cleave to the worship of God; and, indeed, this is mostly the cause of the sufferings of the godly. They will not have to do with that worship that hath sinful traditions commixed with God's appointments, because they know that God is jealous of his worship; and has given a strict charge that all things be done according to the pattern showed to us in the mount. He knows also that God will not be with that worship, and those worshippers, that have not regard to worship by the rule of the testament of Christ. He is also against the sin that is apt to cleave to himself while he standeth in the presence of God. I will wash mine hands in innocency, so will I compass thine altar, O Lord. This man also chooses to be in the practical parts of worship, if possible, for he knows that to have to do about holy things sincerely is the way to be at the remotest distance from sin. He chooses also to be with those holy ones that are of the same mind with him against sin; for he knows that two are better than one, and that a threefold cord is not easily broken. Wherefore look to yourselves, you that do, or may be called to suffer for religion: if you bend not yourselves against sin, if to be revenged of sin be not the cause of your suffering, you cannot be said to suffer for righteousness' sake. Take heed, therefore, that something else be not an inducement to thee to suffer. A man may suffer to save what he has: there is credit also and an applause; there is shame to conform; there is carnal stoutness of spirit; there is hatred of persecutors and scorn to submit; there is fear of contempt and of the reproach of the people, &c. These may be motives and arguments to a suffering state, and may really be the ground of a man's being in the jail; though he cries out in the meanwhile of popery, of superstition, and idolatry, and of the errors that attend the common modes of the religions of the world. I charge no man as though I knew any such thing by any; but I suggest these things as things that are possible, and mention them because I would have sufferers have a care of themselves; and watch and pray, because no man can be upright here that is not holy, that cannot pray, and watch, and deny himself for the love that he has to righteousness. I said it before, and will say it again, it is a rare thing to be set in downrightness of heart against sin.

2. Is it for the sake of righteousness that thou sufferest? Then it is because thou wouldest have righteousness promoted, set up, and established in the world; also thou art afflicted at those advantages that iniquity gets upon men, upon things, and against thyself. "I beheld," said David, "the transgressors, and was grieved; because men kept not thy word" (Psa 119:158). And again, These are they that mourn for the abominations that are done among men (Eze 9:4). There is a great deal of talk about religion, a great deal of pleading for religion, namely, as to the

formalities of this and the other way. But to choose to be religious, that I might be possessed with holiness, and to choose that religion that is most apt to possess me with it, if I suffer for this, I suffer for righteousness' sake. Wherefore say thus to thy soul, thou that art like to suffer for righteousness, How is it with the most inward parts of my soul? What is there? What designs, desires, and reachings out are there? Why do I pray? Why do I read? Why do I hear? Why do I haunt and frequent places and ordinances appointed for worship? Is it because I love holiness? would promote righteousness, because I love to see godliness show itself in others, and because I would feel more of the power of it in myself? If so, and if thou sufferest for thy profession, thou sufferest, not only for righteousness, but also for righteousness' sake. Dost thou thus practise, because thou wouldest be taught to do outward acts of righteousness, and because thou wouldest provoke others to do so too? Dost thou show to others love thou lovest righteousness, by taking opportunities to do righteousness? How is it, dost thou show most mercy to thy dog, or to thine enemy, to thy swine, or to the poor? Whose naked body hast thou clothed? Whose hungry belly hast thou fed? Hast thou taken delight in being defrauded and beguiled? Hast thou willingly sat down by the loss with quietness, and been as if thou hadst not known, when thou hast been wronged, defamed, abused, and all because thou wast not willing that black-mouthed men should vilify and reproach religion upon thy account (1 Cor 6:7)?

He that loveth righteousness will do thus, yea, and do it as unto God, and of tenderness to the Word of God which he professeth. And he that thinks to make seeing men believe, that when he suffereth, he suffereth for righteousness' sake, and yet is void in his life of moral goodness, and that has no heart to suffer and bear, and put up, and pass by injuries in his conversation among his enemies at home, is deceived.

There are some Scriptures that are as if they were out of date among some professors, specially such as call for actual holiness and acts of self-denial for God; but it will be found, at the day of judgment, that they only are the peculiar people that are "zealous of good works" (Titus 2:14). God help us, it is hard now to persuade professors to come up to negative holiness, that is, to leave undone that which is bad; and yet this of itself comes far short of ones being found in practical goodness.

But this is the man that suffereth, when he suffereth for righteousness' sake, that makes it his business, by all lawful means, according to the capacity that God has put him in, to promote, set up, and establish righteousness in the world; I say this is the man that suffereth for righteousness' sake, that suffereth for so doing; and I am sure that a life that is moral, when joined to the profession of the faith of the things that are of the Spirit of God, is absolutely necessary to the promoting of righteousness in the world. Hence Peter tells them that suffer for righteousness' sake, that they must have "a good conscience"—a good conscience towards God, towards men, towards friends, towards enemies (1 Peter 3:14-16; Acts 24:16; 23:1). They must have a good conscience in all things, being willing, ready, desirous to live honestly, godly, and righteously in this world, or else they cannot, though they may suffer for the best doctrine under heaven, suffer for righteousness' sake (Heb 13:18). Wherefore,

3. Is it for righteousness' sake that thou sufferest? then thy design is the ruin of sin. This depends upon what was said before; for he that strives against sin, that seeks to promote righteousness, he designs the ruin of sin. "Be not," said Paul to the suffering Romans, "overcome of evil, but overcome evil with good" (Rom 12:21). To overcome evil with good is a hard task. To rail it down, to cry it down, to pray kings, and parliaments, and men in authority to put it down, this is easier than to use my endeavour to overcome it with good, with doing of good, as I said before. And sin must be overcome with good at home, before thy good can get forth of doors to overcome evil abroad.

Abraham overcame evil with good, when he quieted the discontent of Lot and his herdsmen, with allowing of them to feed their cattle in the best of what God had given him (Gen 13:7,8).

David overcame evil with good, when he saved the life of his bloody enemy that was fallen into his hand; also when he grieved that any hurt should come to them that sought nothing so much as his destruction. "They rewarded me," saith he, "evil for good, to the spoiling of my soul. But as for me, when they were sick, my clothing was sackcloth. I humbled my soul with fasting, I behaved myself as though he had been my friend or brother; I bowed down heavily, as one that mourneth for his mother." This is to overcome evil with good (Psa 35:12-14).

Job saith concerning his enemy, that he did not rejoice when evil found him; "neither have I," said he, "suffered my mouth to sin by wishing a curse to his soul." He means he did the quite contrary, and so overcame evil with good (Job 31:29,30).

Elisha overcame evil with good, when he received the men that came for his life, and had them where he might feast, and comfort them, and sent them home in peace to their master (2 Kings 6:19-23).

The New Testament also is full of this, both in exhortations and examples, In exhortations where it is said, resist not evil, that is, with evil, but overcome evil with good (Prov 24:29). "But whosoever shall smite thee on thy right cheek, turn to him the other also.—And whosoever shall compel thee to go a mile, go with him twain. Give to him that asketh thee; and from him that would borrow of thee, turn not thou away.—Love your enemies, bless them that curse you, do good to them that hate you, and pray for them which despitefully use you, and persecute you; that ye may be the children of your Father which is in heaven, for he maketh his sun to rise on the evil, and on the good - on the just, and on the unjust" (Matt 5:39-45). "Bless them that persecute you: bless and curse not" (Rom 12:14). "Not rendering evil for evil, or railing for railing, but contrariwise, blessing; knowing that ye are thereunto called, that ye should inherit a blessing" (1 Peter 3:9; Rom 12:14). This is righteousness—these are righteous courses. And as these are preceptively propounded, so they were as practically followed by them that were eminently godly in the primitive church.

"We are fools for Christ's sake," said Paul, "we are despised, we are hungry, thirsty, naked, and buffeted.—Being reviled, we bless; being persecuted, we suffer it; being defamed, we entreat: we are made as the filth of the earth, and are the offscouring of all things unto this day" (1 Cor 4:10-13). This is overcoming of evil with good, and he that has chosen to himself that religion that teaches these things, and that loves that religion because it so teacheth him; if he suffereth for it, he suffereth for righteousness' sake.

4. He that suffereth for righteousness' sake, will carry righteousness whithersoever he goes. Neither the enemy, nor thy sufferings, shall be able to take righteousness from thee. Righteousness must be thy chamber mate, thy bed companion, thy walking mate: it is that without which thou wilt be so uncouth, as if thou couldest not live (Psa 26: 25:21).

Paul in his sufferings would have righteousness with him, for it must be as it were his armour-bearer; yea, his very armour itself (2 Cor 6:7). It is an excellent saying of Job, "I put on righteousness, and it clothed me; my judgment was as a robe and a diadem. I was eyes to the blind, and feet was I to the lame; I was a father to the poor," &c. (Job 29:11-16). "Princes," said David also, "did sit and speak against me, but thy servant did meditate in thy statues" (Psa 119:23). A man that loves righteousness doth as Abraham did with his Sarah, carry it every where with him, though he goes, because of that, in danger of his life. Righteousness! It is the only intimate that a Christian has. It is that by which he takes his measures, that with which he consults, with respect to what he doth, or is to do, in the world. "Thy testimonies," said David also, "are my delight, and my counsellors." The men of my counsel, in the margin (Psa 119:24).

David! He was the man of affliction; the suffering man in his day; but in all places where he came, he had righteousness, the law and godly practice with him. It was his counsellor, as he was a man, a saint, a king. I dare say, for the man that suffers righteousness to be rent away from him by the violence and rage of men, and that casts it away, as David did Saul's armour, that he may secure himself; he has no great love for righteousness, nor to the cross for righteousness' sake. "My righteousness I hold fast," said Job, "and will not let it go: my heart shall not reproach me so long as I live" (Job 27:6). What? part with righteousness! A righteous Lord! A righteous Word! A righteous profession! A righteous life! to sleep in a whole skin: the Lord forbid it me, and all that he has counted worthy to be called by his name. Let us carry it with us from the bed to the cross, and then it shall carry us from thence to the crown. Let it be our companion to prison and death, then shall we show that we are lovers of righteousness, and that we choose to suffer for righteousness' sake.

5. Dost thou suffer for righteousness' sake? why then, thy righteousness is not diminished, but rather increased by thy sufferings. Righteousness thriveth best in affliction, the more afflicted, the more holy man; the more persecuted, the more shining man (Acts 6:15). The prison is the furnace, thy graces are the silver and the gold; wherefore, as the silver and the gold are refined by the fire, and so made more to show their native brightness, so the Christian that hath, and that loveth righteousness, and that suffereth for its sake, is by his sufferings refined and made more righteous, and made more Christian, more godly (Zech 13:9). Some, indeed, when they come there, prove lead, iron, tin, and at the best, but the dross of silver; and so are fit for nothing, but there to be left and consumed, and to bear the badge, if ever they come from thence, of reprobate silver from the mouth and sentence of their neighbours (Eze 22:18-22; Jer 6:28-30). But when I, says Job, am tried, "I shall come forth as gold" (Job 23:10).

When Saul had cast one javelin at David, it made him walk wisely in all his ways. But when he added to his first fury, plots to take away his life, then David behaved himself yet more wisely (1 Sam 18:10-30). The hotter the rage and fury of men are against righteous ways, the more those that love righteousness grow therein. For they are concerned for it, not to hide it, but to make it spangle; not to extinguish it, but to greaten it, and to show the excellency of it in all its features, and in all its comely proportion. Now such an one will make straight steps for his feet, "let that which is lame be turned out of the way" (Heb 12:13). Now he shows to all men what faith is, by charity, by self-denial, by meekness, by gentleness, by long-suffering, by patience, by love to enemies, and by doing good to them that hate us; now he walketh upon his high places. Yea, will not now admit that so slovenly a conversation should come within his doors, as did use to haunt his house in former times. Now it is Christmas, now it is suffering time, now we must keep holy day every day. The reason is, for that a man, when he suffereth for Christ, is set upon a hill, upon a stage, as in a theatre, to play a part for God in the world. And you know when men are to play their parts upon a stage, they count themselves, if possible, more bound to circumspection; and that for the credit of their master, the credit of their art, and the credit of themselves. For then the eyes of every body are fixed, they gape and stare upon them (Psa 22:17). And a trip here is as bad as a fall in another place. Also now God himself looks on. Yea, he laugheth, as being pleased to see a good behaviour attending the trial of the innocent.

(1.) He that suffereth for righteousness' sake suffereth for his goodness, and he is now to labour by works and ways to convince the world that he suffereth as such an one. (2.) He that suffereth for righteousness' sake has many that are weak to strengthen by his sweet carriages under the cross, wherefore he had need to exceed in virtue. (3.) He also is by well-doing to put to silence the ignorance of foolish men, he had need be curious and circumspect in all his actions. (4.) He is to come in, and to be a judge, and to condemn, by his faith and patience in his sufferings, the world, with his Lord and fellows, at the appearing of Jesus Christ; he had need be holy himself. This, therefore, is the fit sign of suffering for righteousness' sake (1 Cor 6:1-5; Heb 11:7; 2 Thess 1:5,6; 1 Peter 4:3-5).

6. He that suffereth, not only for righteousness, but also for righteousness' sake, will not exchange his cause, though for it in a jail, for all the ease and pleasure in the world. They that suffered for righteousness' sake of old, were tempted before they were sawn asunder (Heb 11). Tempted, that is, allured, to come out of their present sufferings, and leave their faith and profession in irons behind them. Tempted with promises of promotion, of ease, of friendship, of favour with men. As the Devil said to Christ, so persecutors of old did use to make great promises to sufferers, if they would fall down and worship. But his is alone as if they should say, Butcher, make away with your righteousness, and a good conscience, and you shall find the friendship of the world. For there is no way to kill a man's righteousness but by his own consent. This, Job's wife knew full well, hence she tempted him to lay violent hands upon his own integrity (Job 2:9).

The Devil, nor men of the world can kill thy righteousness or love to it, but by thy own hand; or separate that and thee asunder, without thine own act. Nor will he that doth indeed suffer for the sake of it, or of love he bears thereto, be tempted to exchange it for the goods of all the world. It is a sad sight to see a man that has been suffering for righteousness, restored to his former estate, while the righteousness for which he suffered, remains under locks and irons, and is exposed to the scorn, contempt, reproach of the world, and trodden under the foot of men. "It is better," said Paul, "for me to die, than that any man should make my glorying void." And it had been a hundred times better for that man, if he had never known the way of righteousness, than after he has known it, to turn from the holy commandment delivered unto him.

The striving is, in persecution, for righteousness; to wit, whether it shall be set up, or pulled down. The sufferer, he is for setting up, and the persecutors are for pulling down. Thus they strive for the mastery. Now, if a man stands by his righteousness, and holds fast his good profession, then is righteousness set up; nor can it, so long, be pulled down. Hence, so long a man is said to overcome; and overcome he doth, though he be killed for his profession. But if he starts back, gives place, submits, recants, or denieth any longer to own that good thing that he professed, and exposed himself to suffering for; then he betrays his cause, his profession, his conscience, his righteousness, his soul, and all; for he has delivered up his profession to be murdered before his face: A righteous man falling down before the wicked, is as a troubled fountain, and a corrupt spring (Prov 25:26). But this, I hope, will not he do that loveth righteousness, and that suffereth for righteousness' sake. I do not say but that a man may slip here, with Peter, Origen, Hierom, Cranmer, Baynham, Ormis, and other good folk; but be he one of the right kind, a lover of righteousness indeed, he will return, and take revenge upon himself in a godly way, for so ungodly a fact.

7. He that suffereth not only for righteousness, but also for righteousness sake, is not so wedded

to his own notions as to slight or overlook the good that is in his neighbour. But righteousness he loves wherever he finds it, though it be in him that smiteth him (Psa 141:5). Yea, he will own and acknowledge it for the only thing that is of beauty and glory in the world. With the excellent in the earth is all such a man's delight. Wherefore I put a difference betwixt suffering for an opinion and suffering for righteousness; as I put a difference between suffering for righteousness and suffering for righteousness' sake.

If righteousness, if the stamp of God, if divine authority, is not found upon that thing which I hold, let men never suffer for it under the notion of righteousness. If sin, if superstition, if idolatry, if derogation from the wisdom of Christ, and the authority and perfection of his Word, be not found in, nor joined to that thing that I disown in worship, let me never open my mouth against it. I had rather fall in with, and be an associate of a righteous man that has no true grace, than with a professor that has no righteousness. It is said of the young man, though he went away from Christ, that he looked upon him and loved him (Mark 10:17-22). But it is not said that ever he loved Judas. I know that the righteousness for which a good man suffereth, is not then embraced of the world, for that at such a time it is under a cloud. But yet there is righteousness also in the world, and wherever I see it, it is of a high esteem with me. David acknowledged some of his enemies to be more righteous than he acknowledged some of his servants to be (2 Sam 4:9- 11; 3:31-35). It is a brave thing to have righteousness, as righteousness, to be the top-piece in mine affections. The reason why Christ was anointed with the oil of gladness above his fellows, was, because he loved righteousness, and hated iniquity more than they (Heb. 1:9). Love to righteousness flows from golden graces, and is that, and that only, that can make a man capable of suffering, in our sense, for righteousness' sake.

8. He that suffereth not only for righteousness, but also for righteousness' sake, will take care that his sufferings be so managed with graciousness of words and actions, that it may live when he is dead; yea, and it will please him too, if righteousness flourishes, though by his loss. Hence it is that Paul said, he rejoiced in his suffering, Colossians 1:24; namely, because others got good thereby. And that he said, "Yea, and if I be offered upon the sacrifice and service of your faith, I joy, and rejoice with you all" (Phil 2:17). But why rejoice in this? Why, because though his sufferings were to the distressing of his flesh, yet they were to the refreshing, comfort, and stability of others. This was it also that made him jostle with the false brethren among the churches; to wit, "that the truth of the gospel might continue with them" (Gal 2:5).

When a man shall run the hazard of the ruin of what he has, and is, for righteousness, for the good and benefit of the church of God; that man, he managing himself by the rule, if he suffers for so doing, suffers not only for righteousness, but also for righteousness' sake. "I endure all things," said Paul, "for the elect's sake, that they may also obtain the salvation which is in Christ Jesus with eternal glory" (2 Tim 2:10). Here was love, you will say, to persons; and I will say also, to things; to all the righteousnesses of God that are revealed in the world, that all the elect might enjoy them to their eternal comfort and glory, by Christ Jesus. For "whether we be afflicted," says he, "it is for your consolation and salvation, which is effectual in the enduring of the same sufferings which we also suffer: or whether we be comforted, it is for your consolation and salvation" (2 Cor 1:6).

The end of a man and his design, if that be to promote righteousness, he using lawful means to accomplish it, is greatly accepted of God by Christ; and it is a sign he is a lover of righteousness; and that if he suffereth for so doing, he suffereth not for well-doing, only as to matter of fact, but also for his love to the good thing done, and for its sake.

I have now done with that first head that was to be spoken to, as touching the law and testament, which we have said was to be understood of the will of God spoken of in the text. "Let them that suffer according to the will of God," that is, according to his law and testament. Now we have showed what it is to suffer according to that; we come to another thing, namely:—

[THE WILL OF GOD MEANS HIS ORDER AND DESIGNMENT.]

Second, That by the will of God, we also understand his order and designment. For the will of God is active, to dispose of his people, as well as preceptive, to show unto us our duty. He then that suffers for righteousness' sake, as he suffers for that which is good as to the matter of it, and as he suffers for that which is good, after that manner as becomes that truth for which he suffereth; so he that thus suffereth, suffereth by the order and designment of God. That, then, is the next thing that is to be spoken to, namely:—

God is the great orderer of the battle that is managed in the world against antichrist. Hence that battle is called, "The battle of that great day of God Almighty" (Rev 16:14). It is not what enemies will, nor what they are resolved upon, but what God will, and what God appoints; that shall be done. This doctrine Christ teacheth when he saith, "Are not five sparrows sold for two farthings, and not one of them is forgotten before God? But even the very hairs of your head are all numbered. Fear not therefore: ye are of more value than many sparrows" (Luke 12:6,7). He speaks in the verses before of killing, and bids them that they should not be afraid for that. "Be not afraid of them that kill the body, and after that have no more that they can do. But I will forewarn you whom ye shall fear: Fear him, which after he hath killed hath power to cast into hell; yea, I say unto you, Fear him." Then he leads them to the consideration of this, that the will of God governs, and disposes of his [people] to suffering; as well as declares to them for what, and how they should suffer, saying, "Are not five sparrows sold for two farthings," &c.

Also in Isaiah 8:9,10 and in Isaiah 2:12,13, you have in sum the same thing inserted again. But we will not stay upon proof, but will proceed to demonstration hereof.

Pharaoh said he would, ay, that he would, but he could not touch so much as a thread or a rag of Israel, because the will of God was in that thing contrary to him. Saul said that he would have David, and to that end would search for him among the thousands of Judah; but David was designed for another purpose, and therefore Saul must go without him (1 Sam 23:25) Rabshakeh said that he was come from Assyria to Jerusalem to make "Judah eat their own dung, and drink their own piss" (Isa 36:12). But God said he should not shoot an arrow there. And it came to pass as God had said (Isa 37:33; 2 Kings 18; 2 Chron 28). Jeremiah and Baruch's enemies would have killed them, but they could not, for God hid them. How many times had the Jews a mind to have destroyed Jesus Christ; but they could not touch a hair of his head until his hour was come.

Those also that bound themselves in a curse, that they would neither eat nor drink until they had killed Paul, were forced to be foresworn, for the will of God was not that Paul should die as yet (Acts 23:12). This therefore should be well considered of God's church, in the cloudy and dark day. "All his saints are in thy hand" (Deut 33:3). It is not the way of God to let the enemies of God's church do what they will; no, the Devil himself can devour but "whom he may" (1 Peter 5:8). And as no enemy can bring suffering upon a man when the will of God is otherwise, so no man can save himself out of their hands when God will deliver him up for his glory. It remaineth, then, that we be not much afraid of men, nor yet be foolishly bold; but that we wait upon our God in the way of righteousness, and the use of those means which his providence offereth to us for our safety; and that we conclude that our whole dispose, as to liberty or suffering, lieth in the will of God, and that we shall, or shall not suffer, even as it pleaseth him. For,

First, God has appointed WHO shall suffer. Suffering comes not by chance, or by the will of man, but by the will and appointment of God. "Let no man," said Paul, "be moved by these afflictions; for yourselves know that we are appointed thereunto" (1 Thess 3:3). We are apt to forget God when affliction comes, and to think it a strange thing that those that fear God should suffer indeed (1 Peter 4:12). But we should not, for we suffer by the will and appointment of God. Hence they under the altar were bid to rest for a while, even until their fellow-servants also, and their brethren that should be killed— mark that—"should be killed, as they were, should be fulfilled" (Rev 6:11). Wherefore, suffering for righteousness and for righteousness' sake, is by the will of God. God has appointed who shall suffer. That is the first.

Second, As God has appointed who shall suffer, so he has appointed WHEN they shall suffer for his truth in the world. Sufferings for such and such a man are timed, as to when he shall be tried for his faith. Hence, when Paul was afraid, at Corinth, that the heathens would fall about his ears, the Lord spake to him by night in a vision, saying, "Be not afraid, but speak, and hold not thy peace; for I am with thee, and no man shall set on thee to hurt thee" (Acts 18:9,10). His time of suffering was not yet come there. It is also said concerning Jesus Christ, that even then when "they sought to take him, no man laid hands on him, because his hour was not yet come" (John 7:30). The times, then, and the seasons, even for the sufferings of the people of God, are not in the hands of their enemies, but in the hand of God; as David said, "My times are in thy hand." By the will of God, then, it is that such shall suffer at, but not until, that time. But,

Third, As God has appointed who and when, so he has appointed WHERE this, that, or the other good man shall suffer. Moses and Elias, when they appeared on the holy mount, told Jesus of the sufferings which he should accomplish at Jerusalem. Jerusalem was the place assigned for Christ to suffer at; also, there must the whole of his sufferings be accomplished (Luke 9:30,31). The saints are sprinkled by the hand of God here and there, as salt is sprinkled upon meat to keep it from stinking And as they are thus sprinkled, that they may season the earth; so, accordingly, where they must suffer is also appointed for the better confirming of the truth. Christ said, it could not be that a prophet should "perish out of Jerusalem" (Luke 13:33). But why could it not be that they should perish other where? Were there no enemies but in Jerusalem? Were there no good men but at Jerusalem? No, no; that was not the reason. The reason was, for that God had appointed that they should suffer there. So then, who, when, and where, is at the will of God, and they, accordingly, are ordered by that will.

Fourth, As God has appointed who, when, and where, so he has also appointed WHAT KIND of sufferings this or that saint shall undergo, at this place and at such a time. God said that he would show Paul beforehand how great things he should suffer for his sake (Acts 9:16). And it is said that Christ did signify to Peter beforehand "by what death he should glorify God" (John 21:19). When Herod had beheaded John the Baptist, and when the Jews had crucified Christ, it is said that they had but fulfilled what was "written of them" (Mark 9:13; Acts 13:29). Our sufferings, as to the nature of them, are all writ down in God's book; and though the writing seem as unknown characters to us, yet God understands them very well. Some of them they shall kill and crucify, and some of them they shall scourge in their synagogue, "and persecute them from city to city" (Matt 23:34). Shall God, think you, say, some of them they shall serve thus, and some of them they shall do so to; and yet not allot which some to this, and which to that, and which to the other trial?

Doubtless our sufferings fall by the will of God unto us, as they fell of old upon the people of Jerusalem. It was appointed by God who of them should die of hunger, who with sword, who should go into captivity, and who should be eaten up of beasts (Jer 15:2,3). So is the case here, namely, as God has appointed who, when, where, and the like, so he has, also, what manner of sufferings this or that good man shall undergo for his name. Let it then be concluded, that hitherto it appears, that the sufferings of saints are ordered and disposed by the will of God. But,

Fifth, As all this is determined by the will of God, so it is also appointed FOR WHAT TRUTH this or that saint shall suffer this or that kind of affliction. Every saint has his course, his work, and his testimony, as is allotted him of God (Mark 13:34). John had a course, a testimony to fulfil for God (Acts 13:25), and so had holy Paul (2 Tim 4:6,7), and so has every saint: also, he that is to suffer has his truth appointed him to suffer for. Christ had a truth peculiar to himself to bear witness to in a way of suffering (Mark 14:61,62). John had a truth peculiar to himself to bear witness to in a way of suffering (Mark 6:17,18). Stephen had also a truth, divers from them both, to which he bare a holy testimony, and for which he bravely died (Acts 7:51-53).

If you read the book of Acts and Monuments, you may see a goodly variety as to this; and yet in all a curious harmony. Some are there said to suffer for the Godhead, some for the manhood, some for the ordinances of Christ, and some laid down their lives for the brethren. And thus far we see that he that suffers for righteousness' sake, suffers, in this sense, according to the will of God.

Sixth, As it is appointed who, when, where, what kind, and for what truth, by the will of God, this and that saint should suffer; so also it is appointed BY WHOSE HAND this or that man shall suffer for this or that truth. It was appointed that Moses and Israel should suffer by the hand of Pharaoh. And for this very purpose, said God, have I raised thee up, that is, to be a persecutor, and to reap the fruits thereof (Exo 9:16). It was also determined that Christ should suffer by the hand of Herod and Pontius Pilate; "For of a truth," said they, "against thy holy child Jesus - both Herod, and Pontius Pilate, with the Gentiles, and the people of Israel, were gathered together, for to do whatsoever thy hand and thy counsel determined before to be done" (Acts 4:27).

These are great instances, from which we may gather how all these things are ordered from thence down hitherto. For if a sparrow falls not to the ground without God, she shall not be killed without God; not by he knows not who. And if a Christian man is better than many sparrows, it follows, that God concerns himself more with, for, and about him than with, for, or about many sparrows. It follows, therefore, in right reason, that as the person who is appointed to be the sufferer, so the persons who are appointed to be the rod and sword thereby to afflict withal. Thus far, therefore, the will of God is it that ordereth and disposeth of us and of our sufferings.

Seventh, As all these pass through the hand of God, and come not to us but by his will, so HOW as also LONG is really determined as any of them all. It is not in man, but God, to set the time how long the rod of the wicked shall rest upon the lot of the righteous. Abraham must be informed of this. "Abraham," says God, "know of a surety that thy seed shall be a stranger in a land that is not theirs, and shall serve them; and they shall afflict them four hundred years" (Gen 15:13). So the thraldom of Israel in Babylon was not only in the general appointed, but the time prefixed, how long (Jer 25:11,12; 29:10). The time of the beast's reign and of the witnesses walking in sackcloth are punctually fixed, and that beyond which they cannot go (Rev 11, 12, 13).

I know these are generals, and respect the church in the bulk of it, and not particular persons. But, as was hinted afore, we must argue from the greater to the lesser, that is, from four hundred years to ten days, from ten days to three, and so from the church in general to each particular member, and to the time and nature of their sufferings (Rev 2:10; Hosea 6:2; Acts 23:11).

And thus, in a word or two, I have finished the first two parts of the text, and showed you what there is in Peter's counsel and advice; and showed you also, to whom his advice is given: in which last, as you see, I have showed you both what the will of God is, and what to suffer according to it. And particularly, I have, in a few words, handled this last, to show you that our imprisonment was appointed and disposed by him, that you might always, when you come into trouble for his name, not stagger nor be at a loss, but be stayed, composed, and settled in your minds, and say, "The will of the Lord be done" (Acts 21:14). I will also say unto you this by the way, that the will of God doth greatly work, even to order and dispose of the spirits of Christians, in order to willingness, disposedness, readiness, and resignation of ourselves to the mind of God. For with respect to this were those words last recited spoken. Paul saw that he had a call to go up to Jerusalem, there to bear his testimony for Christ and his gospel; but those unto whom he made know his purpose entreated him, with much earnestness, not to go up thither, for that, as they believed, it would endanger his life. But he answereth, What, mean ye to weep, and to break my heart? for I am ready, not to be bound only, but also to die at Jerusalem for the name of the Lord Jesus. And when he would not be persuaded, says Luke, we ceased, saying, "The will of the Lord be done."
From what has been thus discoursed, many things will follow; as,

1. That the rod, as well as the child, is God's; persecutors, as well as the persecuted, are his, and he has his own designs upon both. He has raised them up, and he has ordered them for himself, and for that work that he has for them to do. Hence Habakkuk, speaking of the church's enemies, saith, "Thou hast ordained them for judgment; and, O mighty God, thou hast established them for correction" (Hab 1:12). And, therefore, they are in other places called the rod of God's anger; his staff (Isa 10:5), his hand; his sword (Psa 17:13,14).

Indeed, to be thus disposed of, is a sad lot; the lot is not fallen to them in pleasant places, they have not the goodly heritage; but the judgments of God are a great deep. The thing formed may not say to him that formed it, Why hast thou made me thus? To be appointed, to be ordained, to be established to be a persecutor, and a troubler of God's church—O tremendous judgment! O amazing anger!

Three things the people of God should learn from hence.

(1.) Learn to pity and bewail the condition of the enemy; I know thou canst not alter the counsel of God; appointed they are, established they are for their work, and do it they must and shall. But yet it becomes them that see their state, and that their day is coming, to pity and bewail their condition, yea, and to pray for them too; for who knows whether it is determined that they should remain implacable to the end, as Herod; or whether they may through grace obtain repentance of their doings, with Saul. And I say again, if thy prayer should have a casting hand in the conversion of any of them, it would be sweet to thy thoughts when the scene is over.

(2.) Never grudge them their present advantages. "Fret not thyself because of evil men, neither be thou envious at the workers of iniquity" (Prov 24:19). Fret not, though they spoil thy resting-place. It is God that has bidden them do it, to try thy faith and patience thereby. Wish them no ill with what they get of thine; it is their wages for their work, and it will appear to them ere long that they have earned it dearly. Their time is to rejoice but as in a moment, in what thus is gotten by them; and then they, not repenting, are to perish for ever, like their own dung (Job 20:5-7). Poor man, thou that hast thy time to be afflicted by them, that thy golden graces may shine the more, thou art in the fire, and they blow the bellows. But wouldest thou change places with them? Wouldest thou sit upon their place of ease? Dost thou desire to be with them (Prov 24:1)? O rest thyself contented; in thy patience possess thy soul, and pity and bewail them in the condition in which they are.

(3.) Bless God that thy lot did fall on the other side, namely, to be one that should know the truth, profess it, suffer for it, and have grace to bear thee up thereunder, to God's glory, and thy eternal comfort. This honour have not all his saints; all are not counted worthy thus to suffer shame for his name. Do this, I say, though they get all, and leave thee nothing but the shirt on thy back, the skin on thy bones, or an hole in the ground to be put in (Heb 11:23-26).

2. Labour to be patient under this mighty hand of God, and be not hasty to say, When will the rod be laid aside? mind thou thy duty, which is to let patience have its perfect work. And bear the indignation of the Lord, because thou hast sinned against him, until he please to awake, to arise, and to execute judgment for thee (Micah 7:9). But to pass this.
Are things thus ordered? then this should teach us that there is a cause.
The rod is not gathered without a cause; the rod is fore- determined, because the sin of God's people is foreseen, and ofttimes the nature of the sin, and the anger of the Father, is seen in the fashion of the rod. The rod of my anger, saith God. A bitter and hasty nation must be brought against Jerusalem; an enemy fierce and cruel must be brought against the land of Israel. Their sins called for such a rod, for their iniquities were grievous (Hab 1:6).

This should teach us with all earnestness to be sorry for our sins, and to do what we can to prevent these things, by falling upon our face in a way of prayer before God. If we would shorten such days, when they come upon us, let us be lovers of righteousness, and get more of the righteousness of faith, and of compliance with the whole will of God into our hearts. Then I say, the days shall be shortened, or we fare as well, because the more harmless and innocent we are, and suffer, the greater will our wages, our reward, and glory be, when pay-day shall come; and what if we wait a little for that?

These things are sent to better God's people, and to make them white, to refine them as silver, and to purge them as gold, and to cause that they that bear some fruit, may bring forth more: we are afflicted, that we may grow (John 15:2). It is also the will of God, that they that go to heaven should go thither hardly or with difficulty. The righteous shall scarcely be saved. That is, they shall, but yet with great difficulty, that it may be the sweeter.

Now that which makes the way to heaven so strait, so narrow, so hard, is the rod, the sword the persecutor, that lies in the way, that marks where our haunt is, that mars our path, digs a pit, and that acts a net, a snare for us in the way (1 Sam 23:22; Job 30:12-14; Psa 9:15; 31:4; 35:7; 119:110; 140:5; 142:3).

This, I say, is that which puts us to it, but it is to try, as I said, our graces, and to make heaven the sweeter to us. To come frighted and hard pursued thither, will make the safety there the more with exceeding gladness to be embraced. And I say, get thy heart yet more possessed with the power of godliness; that the love of righteousness may be yet more with thee. For this blessedness, this happiness, he shall be sure of, that suffereth for righteousness' sake.

3. Since the rod is God's as well as the child, let us not look upon our troubles as if they came from, and were managed only by hell. It is true, a persecutor has a black mark upon him, but yet the Scriptures say that all the ways of the persecutor are God's (Dan 5:23). Wherefore as we should, so again we should not, be afraid of men: we should be afraid of them, because they will hurt us; but we should not be afraid of them, as if they were let loose to do to us, and with us, what they will. God's bridle is upon them, God's hook is in their nose: yea, and God has determined the bounds of their rage, and if he lets them drive his church into the sea of troubles, it shall be but up to the neck, and so far it may go, and not be drowned (2 Kings 19:28; Isa 37:29; 8:7,8). I say the Lord has hold of them, and orders them; nor do they at any time come out against his people but by his licence and commission how far to go, and where to stop. And now for two or three objections:—

1. Object. But may we not fly in a time of persecution? Your pressing upon us, that persecution is ordered and managed by God, makes us afraid to fly.

Answ. First, having regard to what was said afore about a call to suffer; thou mayest do in this even as it is in thy heart. If it is in thy heart to fly, fly: if it be in thy heart to stand, stand. Any thing but a denial of the truth. He that flies, has warrant to do so; he that stands, has warrant to do so. Yea, the same man may both fly and stand, as the call and working of God with his heart may be. Moses fled (Exo 2:15), Moses stood (Heb 11:27). David fled (1 Sam 19:12), David stood

(24:8). Jeremiah fled (Jer 37:11,12), Jeremiah stood (38:17). Christ withdrew himself (Luke 9:10), Christ stood (John 18:1-8). Paul fled (2 Cor 11:33), Paul stood (Acts 20:22,23).

There are therefore few rules in this case. The man himself is best able to judge concerning his present strength, and what weight this or that argument has upon his heart to stand or fly. I should be loath to impose upon any man in these things; only, if thou fliest, take two or three cautions with thee:—

(1.) Do not fly out of a slavish fear, but rather because flying is an ordinance of God, opening a door for the escape of some, which door is opened by God's providence, and the escape countenanced by God's Word (Matt 10:23).

(2.) When thou art fled, do as much good as thou canst in all quarters where thou comest, for therefore the door was opened to thee, and thou bid to make thy escape (Acts 8:1-5).

(3.) Do not think thyself secure when thou art fled; it was providence that opened the door, and the Word that did bid thee escape: but whither, and wherefore, that thou knowest not yet. Uriah the prophet fled into Egypt, because there dwelt men that were to take him, that he might be brought again to Jerusalem to die there (Jer 26:21).

(4.) Shouldest thou fly from where thou art, and be taken in another place; the most that can be made of it—thy taking the opportunity to fly, as was propounded at first—can be but this, thou wast willing to commit thyself to God in the way of his providence, as other good men have done, and thy being now apprehended has made thy call clear to suffer here or there, the which before thou wert in the dark about.

(5.) If, therefore, when thou hast fled, thou art taken, be not offended at God or man: not at God, for thou art his servant, thy life and thy all are his; not at man, for he is but God's rod, and is ordained, in this, to do thee good. Hast thou escaped? Laugh. Art thou taken? Laugh. I mean, be pleased which way soever things shall go, for that the scales are still in God's hand.

(6.) But fly not, in flying, from religion; fly not, in flying, for the sake of a trade; fly not, in flying, that thou mayest have ease for the flesh: this is wicked, and will yield neither peace nor profit to thy soul; neither now, nor at death, nor at the day of judgment.

2. Object. But if I fly, some will blame me: what must I do now?

Answ. And so many others if thou standest; fly not, therefore, as was said afore, out of a slavish fear; stand not, of a bravado. Do what thou dost in the fear of God, guiding thyself by his Word and providence; and as for this or that man's judgment, refer thy case to the judgment of God.

3. Object. But if I be taken and suffer, my cause is like to be clothed with scandals, slanders, reproaches, and all manner of false, and evil speakings; what must I do?

Answ. Saul charged David with rebellion (1 Sam 22:8,13). Amos was charged with conspiring against the king (Amos 7:10). Daniel was charged with despising the king; and so also were the three children (Dan 6:13; 3:12). Jesus Christ himself was accused of perverting the nation, of forbidding to give tribute to Caesar, and of saying that himself was Christ a king (Luke 23:2). These things therefore have been. But,

(1.) Canst thou, after a due examination of thyself, say that as to these things thou art innocent and clear? I say, will thy conscience justify thee here? Hast thou made it thy business to give unto God the things that are God's, and unto Caesar the things that are his, according as God has commanded? If so, matter not what men shall say, nor with what lies and reproaches they slander thee, but for these things count thyself happy. Blessed are ye, when men shall revile you - and shall say all manner of evil against you falsely (lying) for my sake (saith Christ). Rejoice, and be exceeding glad: for great is your reward in heaven: for so persecuted they the prophets which were before you (Matt 5:11,12). Comfort thyself therefore in the innocency of thy soul, and say, I am counted a rebel, and yet am loyal; I am counted a deceiver, and yet am true (1 Sam 24:8-12, 2 Cor 6:8). Also refer thy cause to the day of judgment; for if thou canst rejoice at the thoughts that thou shalt be cleared of all slanders and evil speakings then, that will bear up thy heart as to what thou mayest suffer now. The answer of a good conscience will carry a man through hell to heaven. Count these slanders part of thy sufferings, and those for which God will give thee a reward, because thou art innocent, and for that they are laid upon thee for thy profession's sake. But if thou be guilty, look to thyself; I am no comforter of such.

[THIRD, THE GOOD EFFECT OF COMMITTING THE SOUL TO GOD'S KEEPING.]

I come now to speak to the third and last part of the text, namely, of the good effect that will certainly follow to those that, after a due manner, shall take the advice afore given. "Let them that suffer according to the will of God, commit the keeping of their souls to him in well-doing, as unto a faithful Creator."

Two things from the last clause of the text lie yet before us. And they are they by which will be shown what good effect will follow to those that suffer according to the will of God, and that commit their souls to his keeping. 1. Such will find him to themselves a Creator. 2. They will find him a faithful Creator. "Let them commit the keeping of their souls to him, as unto a faithful Creator."

In this phrase, a Faithful Creator, behold the wisdom of the Holy Ghost, how fitly and to the purpose he speaketh. King is a great title, and God is sometimes called a King; but he is not set forth by this title here, but by the title of a Creator; for it is not always in the power of a king to succour and relieve his subjects, that are suffering for his crown and dignity. Father is a sweet title—a title that carrieth in it an intimation of a great deal of bowels and compassion, and God is often set forth also by this title in the holy Scriptures. But so he is not here, but rather as a Creator. For a father, a compassionate father, cannot always help, succour, or relieve his children, though he knows they are under affliction! Oh! but a Creator can. Wherefore, I say, he is set forth here under the title of Creator.

FIRST, A Creator! nothing can die under a Creator's hands. A Creator can sustain all. A Creator can, as a Creator, do what he pleases. "The Lord, the everlasting God, the Creator of the ends of the earth, fainteth not, neither is weary" (Isa 40:28).

The cause of God, for which his people suffer, had been dead and buried a thousand years ago, had it not been in the hand of a Creator. The people that have stood by his cause had been out of both as to persons, name, and remembrance, had they not been in the hand of a Creator. Who could have hoped, when Israel was going in, even into the mouth of the Red Sea, that ever his cause, or that people, should have revived again. A huge host of the Egyptians were behind them, and nothing but death before and on every hand of them; but they lived, they flourished, they outlived their enemies, for they were in the hand of a Creator.

Who could have hoped that Israel should have returned again from the land, from the hand, and from under the tyranny of the king of Babylon? They could not deliver themselves from going thither, they could not preserve themselves from being diminished when they came there, their power was gone, they were in captivity, their distance from home was far, their enemies possessed their land, their city of defence was ruined, and their houses burned down to the ground; and yet they came home again: there is nothing impossible to a Creator.

Who could have thought that the three children could have lived in a fiery furnace? that Daniel could have been safe among the lions? that Jonah could have come home to his country, when he was in the whale's belly? or that our Lord should have risen again from the dead? But what is impossible to a Creator?

This, therefore, is a rare consideration for those to let their hearts be acquainted with that suffer according to the will of God, and that have committed the keeping of their souls to him in well-doing. They have a Creator to maintain and uphold their cause, a Creator to oppose its opposers. And hence it is said, all that burden themselves with Jerusalem "shall be cut in pieces, though all the people of the earth be gathered together against it" (Zech 12:3).

SECOND, A Creator! A Creator can not only support a dying cause, but also fainting spirits. For as he fainteth not, nor is weary, so "he giveth power to the faint, and to them that have no might he increaseth strength" (Isa 40:29). He is the God of the spirits of all flesh, and has the life of the spirit of his people in his own hand. Spirits have their being from him; he is the Father of spirits. Spirits are made strong by him, nor can any crush that spirit that God the Creator will uphold.

Is it not a thing amazing to see one poor inconsiderable man, in a spirit of faith and patience, overcome all the threatenings, cruelties, afflictions, and sorrows, that a whole world can lay upon him? None can quail him, none can crush him, none can bend down his spirit. None can make him to forsake what he has received of God—a commandment to hold fast. His holy, harmless, and profitable notions, because they are spiced with grace, yield to him more comfort, joy, and peace, and do kindle in his soul so goodly a fire of love to, and zeal for God, that all the waters of the world shall not be able to quench.

Ay, say some, that is because his is headstrong, obstinate, and one that will hear no reason. No, say I, but it is because his spirit is in the hand, under the conduct and preservation, of a Creator. A Creator can make spirits, uphold spirits, and make one spirit stronger to stand, than are all the spirits of the world to cast down. To stand, I say, in a way of patient enduring in well-doing, against all that hell can do to suppress.

THIRD, A Creator! A Creator can bring down the spirits that oppose, and make them weak and unstable as water. The Lord, the everlasting God, the Creator of the ends of the earth, fainteth not, nor is weary; there is no searching of his understanding. He gives power to the faint, and to those that have no might, he increaseth strength; now mark, even the young shall faint and be weary, and the young men shall utterly fall. A Creator can dash the spirits of the enemies with fear. God can put them in fear, and make them know that they are men and not God, and that their horses are flesh and not spirit. When the enemy came to take Jesus Christ, their spirits fainted, their hearts died in them; they went backwards, and fell to the ground. They had hard work to strengthen their spirits to a sufficiency of boldness and courage, though they brought halberts, and staves, and swords, and weapons with them, to take a naked man (John 18:3-7).

And although this is that which is not so visible to the world as some other things are, yet I believe that God treads down the spirits of men in a day when they afflict his people, oftener than we are aware of, or than they are willing to confess. How was the hostile spirit of Esau trod down of God, when he came out to meet his poor naked brother, with no less than four hundred armed men? He fainted before his brother, and instead of killing, kissed him (Gen 33:4). How was the bloody spirit of Saul trod down, when David met him at the mouth of the cave, and also at the hill Hachilah (1 Sam 24; 26)? God is a Creator, and as a Creator, is a spirit maker, a spirit reviver, a spirit destroyer; he can destroy body and soul in hell (Luke 12:5).

FOURTH, A Creator! As a Creator, he is over all arts, inventions, and crafts of men that are set on work to destroy God's people, whether they be soldiers, excellent orators, or any other whatsoever; we will single out one—the smith, that roaring fellow, who with his coals and his bellows makes a continual noise. "I have created the smith," said God, "that bloweth the coals in the fire, and that bringeth forth an instrument for his work; and I have created the waster to destroy" (Isa 54:16). The smith, what is he? I answer, an idol maker, a promoter of false worship, and one that makes instruments of cruelty, therewith to help to suppress the true [worship] (Isa 41:7; 44:12; 46:6).

"I have created the smith," saith God, "that bloweth the coals in the fire." The idol inventor, the idol maker, the supporter of idol worship, he is my creature, saith God, to teach that he has power to reach him, and to command his sword to approach him at his pleasure, notwithstanding his roaring with his bellows, and his coals in the fire. So then, he cannot do what he will in the fire, nor with his idol when he has made it; the instrument, also that he makes for the defence of his idol, and for the suppressing of God's true worship, shall not do the thing for the which it is designed by him. And so the very next verse saith: "No weapon that is formed against thee shall prosper, and every tongue that shall rise against thee in judgment thou shalt condemn. This is the heritage of the servants of the Lord, and their righteousness is of me, saith the Lord" (Isa 54:17). And the text saith moreover, I have created the waster to destroy. The waster, what is that? Why, the smith makes an idol, and God has made the rust; the smith makes a sword, and God has made the rust. The rust eats them up, the moth shall eat them up, the fire shall devour them. "The wicked," saith the Psalmist, "have drawn out the sword, and have bent their bow, to cast down the poor and needy, and to slay such as be of upright conversation. Their sword shall enter into their own heart, and their bows shall be broken" (Psa 37:14,15).

All this can God do, because he is a Creator, and none but God can do it. Wherefore by this peculiar title of Creator, the apostle prepareth support for suffering saints, and also shows what a good conclusion is like to be made with them that suffer for righteousness' sake, according to his will; and that commit the keeping of their souls to him in well-doing, as unto a faithful Creator.

FIFTH, A Creator! A Creator can make such provision for a suffering people, in all respects, as shall answer all their wants. Have they lost their peace with the world? Have they no more peace with this world? Why, a Creator can make, create peace, can create peace, peace; peace with God, and peace with his conscience; and that is better than all the peace that can be found elsewhere in the world (Isa 57:19). Have they lost a good frame of heart? Do they want a right frame of spirit? Why, though this is to be had no where in the world, yet a Creator can help them to it (Psa 51:10). Have they lost their spiritual defence? Do they lie too open to their spiritual foes? Why, this a Creator can help. "And the Lord will create upon every dwelling place of Mount Zion, and upon her assemblies, a cloud and smoke by day, and the shining of a flaming fire by night: for upon all the glory shall be a defence." (Isa 4:5)

This is the work of the Spirit; for though the Spirit itself be uncreated, yet all the holy works of it in the heart are verily works of creation. Our new man is a creation; our graces are a creation; our joys and comforts are a creation (2 Cor 5:17,18; Eph 4:24; Isa 65:17-19). Now a creation none can destroy but a Creator; wherefore here is comfort. But again, God hath created us in Christ Jesus; that is another thing. The sun is created in the heavens; the stars are created in the heavens; the moon is created in the heavens. Who can reach them, touch them, destroy them, but the Creator? Why, this is the case of the saint; because he has to do with a Creator, he is fastened to Christ; yea, is in him by an act of creation (Eph 2:10), so that unless Christ and the creation of the Holy Ghost can be destroyed, he is safe that is suffering according to the will of God, and that hath committed the keeping of his soul to him in well-doing, as unto a faithful Creator. And this I would have you consider moreover; the man that suffereth according to the will of God committeth not only a soul to this Creator as dwells in carnal men—a naked soul, a graceless soul, a soul that has nothing in it but sin, but he commits a converted soul, a regenerate soul, a soul adorned, beautified, and sanctified, with the jewels, and bracelets, earrings, and perfumes of the blessed Spirit of grace. And I say again, this is the work of a Creator, and a Creator can maintain it in its gallantry,

FOOTNOTE? "Gallantry"; splendour of appearance, grandeur, nobleness.—Ed.

and he will do so, but he will put forth acts of creating power for it every day.

SIXTH, A Creator! He that can create can turn and alter any thing, to what himself would have it. He that made "the seven stars and Orion, and turneth the shadow of death into the morning" (Amos 5:8), he can "make the wilderness a pool of water, and the dry land springs of water" (Isa 41:18). Our most afflicted and desolate conditions, he can make as a little haven unto us; he can make us sing in the wilderness, and can give us our vineyards from thence (Hosea 2:14,15). He can make Paul sing in the stocks, and good Rowland Taylor dance as he goeth to the burning stake. Jails, and mocks, and scourgings, and flouts and imprisonments, and hunger, and nakedness, and peril, and sword, and dens, and caves, and rocks, and mountains, God can so sweeten with the honey of his Word, and make so famous for situation by the glory of his presence, and so rich and fruitful by the communications of the Holy Ghost, and so easy by the spreading of his feathers over us, that we shall not be able to say, that in all the world a more commodious place, or comfortable condition, can be found. Some have know this, and have been rather ready to covet to be here, than to shun and fly from it, as a most unsavoury condition.

All these things, I say, God doth as a Creator. He hath created antipathies, and he can make antipathies close, and have favour one for another. The lion and the calf, the wolf and the lamb, the little boy and the cockatrice's den he can reconcile, and make to be at agreement. So, sufferings and the saint; the prison and the saint; losses, crosses, and afflictions, and the saint: he can make to lie down sweetly together.

SEVENTH, A Creator! A Creator can make up all that thou hast or shalt lose for the sake of thy profession by the hands of the children of men, be they friends, relations, a world, life, or what you can conceive of.

1. Hast thou lost thy friend for the sake of thy profession? Is the whole world set against thee for thy love to God, to Christ, his cause, and righteousness? Why, a Creator can make up all. Here, therefore, is the advantage that he hath that suffereth for righteousness' sake. Jonathan, the very son of bloody Saul, when David had lost the help of all his own relations, he must fall in with him, stick to him, and love him as he loved his own soul (1 Sam 18:1-3). Obadiah, Ahab's steward, when the saints were driven even under ground by the rage of Jezebel the queen, he is appointed of God to feed them in caves and holes of the earth (1 Kings 18:13). Yea, the very raven complied with the will of a Creator to bring the prophet bread and flesh in the morning, and bread and flesh at night (17:6). When Jeremiah the prophet was rejected of all, yea, the church that then was, could not help him; he was cast into the dungeon, and sunk to a great depth there in the mire. God the Creator, who ruleth the spirits of all men, stirred up the heart of Ebed-melech the Ethiopian both to petition for his liberty, and to put him out of the dungeon by the help of thirty men (Jer 38:7-13). These now, as Christ says, were both fathers, mothers, brothers, sisters, and as a loving wife or child (Matt 19:29).

2. Hast thou, for the sake of thy faith and profession thereof, lost thy part in the world? Why, a Creator can make thee houses as he did for the midwives of Egypt (Exo 1:20,21), and can build thee a sure house as he did for David his servant, who ventured all for the love that they had to the fear of God and his way (2 Sam 7). David was thrust out of Saul's house, and driven from his own, and God opened the heart of Achisch the king of Gath to receive him, and to give him Ziklag. David, when under the tyranny of Saul, knew not what to do with his father and his mother, who were persecuted for his sake, but a Creator inclined the heart of the king of Moab to receive them to house and harbour (1 Sam 27:5; 22:3,4).

3. Is thy life at stake—is that like to go for thy profession, for thy harmless profession of the gospel? Why, God the Creator is Lord of life, and to God the Lord belong the issues from death. So then, he can, if he will, hold thy breath in thy nostrils, in spite of all the world; or if he shall suffer them to take away this for his glory, he can give thee another ten times as good for thy comfort. "He that loveth his life shall lose it; and he that hateth his life in this world shall keep it unto life eternal" (John 12:25).

4. Is thy body to be disfigured, dismembered, starved, hanged, or burned for the faith and profession of the gospel? Why, a Creator can either prevent it, or, suffering it, can restore it the very same to thee again, with great and manifold advantage. He that made thee to be now what thou art, can make thee to be what thou never yet wast. It doth not yet appear what we shall be, further than only by general words (1 John 3:2; Phil 3:21).

EIGHTH, A Creator! Peter sets him before us here as a Creator, because he would have us live upon him as such; as well as upon his grace, love, and mercy. In Job's day this was bewailed, that none or but a few said, "Where is God my maker, who giveth songs in the night?" (Job 35:10).

Creator, as was hinted before, is one of God's peculiar titles. It is not given to him above five or six times in all the Book of God; and usually, when given him, it is either to show his greatness, or else to convince us that of duty we ought to depend upon him; and not to faint, if he be on our side, for or under any adversity, according as we are bidden in the text: "Let them that suffer according to the will of God, commit the keeping of their souls to him in well doing, as unto a faithful creator." Shall God display his glory before us under the character and title of a Creator, and shall we yet fear man? Shall he do this to us when we are under a suffering condition, and that on purpose that we might commit our souls to him in well- doing, and be quiet, and shall we take no notice of this? "Who art thou, that thou shouldest be afraid of a man that shall die, and of the son of man which shall be made as grass; and forgettest the Lord thy maker, that hath stretched forth the heavens, and laid the foundations of the earth?" &c. (Isa 51:12,13).

Had God concealed himself, as to his being a Creator, yet since he presenteth himself unto us by his Word under so many excellent titles as are given to no other God besides, methinks it should make us bold in our God; but when, for our relief, he shall add to all other that he verily is a Creator, this should make us rest in hope indeed.

Every nation will have confidence for their own gods, though but gods that are made with hands—though but the work of the smith and carpenter; and shall not we trust in the name of the Lord our God, who is not only a God, but a Creator and former of all things (Micah 4:5), consequently, the only living and true God, and one that alone can sustain us? We therefore are to be greatly blamed if we overlook the ground, such ground of support and comfort as presenteth itself unto us under the title of a Creator; but then most of all, if, when we have heard, believed, and known that our God is such, we shall yet be afraid of a man that shall die, and forget the Lord our maker. We, I say, have heard, seen, known, and believed, that our God is the Creator. The heavens declare his glory, and the firmament showeth his handy-work, and thus he has showed unto us "his eternal power and Godhead" (Rom 1:20).

Behold, then, thou fearful worm, Jacob, the heavens, the sun, the moon, the stars; behold the earth, the sea, the air, the fire, and vapours. Behold, all living things, from leviathan and behemoth to the least that creepeth in the earth and waters. Yea, behold thyself, thy soul, thy body, thy fashion, thy building, and consider; thy God hath made even all these things, and hath given to thee this being; yea, and all this also he made of that which doth not appear (Heb 11:1-3). This is that which thou art called to the consideration of by Peter, in the text; when he letteth fall from his apostolical meditation that thy God is the Creator, and commandeth that thou, in thy suffering for him according to his will, shouldest commit the keeping of thy soul to him as unto a faithful Creator.

He that has the art thus to do, and that can do it in his straits, shall never be trodden down. His God, his faith; his faith, his God, are able to make him stand. For such a man will thus conclude, that since the Creator of all is with him, what but creatures are there to be against him? So, then, what is the axe, that it should boast itself against him that heweth therewith? or the saw, that it should magnify itself against him that shaketh it? as if the rod should shake itself against him that lifteth it up; or as if the staff should lift up itself as if it were not wood (Isa 10:15). Read also Isaiah 40:12-31, and then speak, if God as Creator is not a sure confidence to all the ends of the earth that trust in, and wait upon him. As Creator, he hath formed and upholdeth all things; yea, his hands have formed the crooked serpent, wherefore he also is at his bay (Job 26:13). And thou hast made the dragon in the sea; and therefore it follows that he can cut and wound him (Isa 51:9), and give him for meat to the fowls, and to the beasts inheriting the wilderness (Psa 74:13,14), if he will seek to swallow up and destroy the church and people of God (Eze 29:3,4).

NINTH, A Creator is God! the God unto whom they that suffer according to his will are to commit the keeping of their souls— the Creator. And doth he take charge of them as a Creator? Then this should teach us to be far off from being dismayed, as the heathens are, at his tokens; for our God, the Lord, is the true God, the living God, the King of eternity (Jer 10:1,2,10). We should tremblingly glory and rejoice when we see him in the world, though upon those that are the most terrible of his dispensations. God the Creator will sometimes mount himself and ride through the earth in such majesty and glory, that he will make all to stand in the tent doors to behold him. O how he rode in his chariots of salvation when he went to save his people out of the land of Egypt! How he shook the nations! Then "his glory covered the heavens, and the earth was full of his praise. And his brightness was as the light; he had horns coming out of his hand: and there was the hiding of his power. Before him went the pestilence, and burning coals went forth at his feet. He stood, and measured the earth: he beheld, and drove asunder the nations; and the everlasting mountains were scattered, the perpetual hills did bow: his ways are everlasting." Then said the prophet, "I saw the tents of Cushan in affliction: and the curtains of the land of Midian did tremble. Was the Lord displeased against the rivers? was thine anger against the rivers? was thy wrath against the sea, that thou didst ride upon thine horses and thy chariots of salvation?" (Hab 3:3-8).

So David: "The earth shook and trembled," said he; "the foundations also of the hills moved and were shaken, because he was wroth. There went up a smoke out of his nostrils, and fire out of his mouth devoured: coals were kindled by it. He bowed the heavens also, and came down: and darkness was under his feet. And he rode upon a cherub, and did fly: yea, he did fly upon the wings of the wind. He made darkness his secret place; his pavilion round about him were dark waters and thick clouds of the skies. At the brightness that was before him his thick clouds passed, hail stones and coals of fire. The Lord also thundered in the heavens, and the Highest gave his voice; hail stones and coals of fire. Yea, he sent out his arrows, and scattered them; and he shot out lightnings, and discomfited them. Then the channels of waters were seen, and the foundations of the world were discovered at thy rebuke, O Lord, at the blast of the breath of thy nostrils" (Psa 18:7-15).

These are glorious things, though shaking dispensations. God is worthy to be seen in his dispensations as well as in his Word, though the nations tremble at his presence. "Oh that thou wouldest rend the heavens, that thou wouldest come down," saith the prophet, "that the mountains might flow down at thy presence!" (Isa 64:1). We know God, and he is our God, our own God of whom it is of what should we be afraid? (Psa 46). When God roars out of Zion, and utters his voice from Jerusalem, when the heavens and the earth do shake, the Lord shall be the hope of his people, and the strength of the children of Israel (Joel 3:16).

Every man stayeth up, or letteth his spirit fail, according to what he knoweth concerning the nature of a thing. He that knows the sea, knows the waves will toss themselves: he that knows a lion, will not much wonder to see his paw, or to hear the voice of his roaring. And shall we that know our God be stricken with a panic fear, when he cometh out of his holy place to punish the inhabitants of the earth for their iniquity? We should stand like those that are next to angels, and tell the blind world who it is that is thus mounted upon his steed, and that hath the clouds for the dust of his feet, and that thus rideth upon the wings of the wind: we should say unto them, "This God is our God for ever and ever, and he shall be our guide even unto death."

Our God! the Creator! He can turn men to destruction, and say, Return, ye children of men. When our God shows himself, it is worth the while to see the sight, though it costs us all that we have to behold it. Some men will bless and admire every rascally juggler that can but make again that which they only seem to mar, or do something that seems to outgo reason; yea, though they make thunderings and noise in the place where they are, as though the devil himself were there. Shall saints, then, like slaves, be afraid of their God, the Creator; of their own God, when he rendeth the heavens, and comes down? When God comes into the world to do great things, he must come like himself—like him that is a Creator: wherefore the heavens and the earth must move at his presence, to signify that they acknowledge him as such, and pay him that homage that is due to him as their God and great Creator.

We that are Christians have been trained up by his Son in his school this many a day, and have been told what a God our Father is, what an arm he has, and with what a voice he can thunder; how he can deck himself with majesty and excellency, and array himself with beauty and glory; how he can cast abroad the rage of his wrath, and behold every one that is proud, and abase him (Job 40:9-11). Have we not talked of what he did at the Red Sea, and in the land of Ham many years ago, and have we forgot him now? Have we not vaunted and boasted of our God both in church, pulpit, and books; and spake to the praise of them that, instead of stones, attempted to drive antichrist out of the world with their lives and their blood; and are we afraid of our God? He was God, a Creator, then; and is he not God now? and will he not be as good to us as to them that have gone before us? or would we limit him to appear in such ways as only smile upon our flesh; and have him stay, and not show himself in his heart-shaking dispensations until we are dead and gone? What if we must go now to heaven, and what if he is thus come down to fetch us to himself? If we have been wise as serpents, and innocent as doves—if we can say, Neither against the law of the Jews, neither against the temple, nor against Caesar, have we offended anything at all, of what should we be afraid? Let heaven and earth come together, I dare say they will not hurt us.

Our Lord Jesus, when dilating upon some of the great and necessary works of our Creator, puts check beforehand to all uncomely fears; to such fears as become not the faith and profession of a Christian. "Brother," saith he, "shall deliver up the brother to death, and the father the child: and the children shall rise up against their parents, and cause them to be put to death. And ye shall be hated of all men for my name's sake." What follows? (verse 28), "Fear them not"; and again, in verse 31, "Fear ye not" (Matt 10:21,22).

So again (Matt 24): "Nation shall rise against nation - there shall be famines, pestilences, and earthquakes, &c. They shall deliver you up to be afflicted, and shall kill you.—Many shall be offended, and shall betray one another.—And many false prophets shall arise, and deceive many." And yet for all this we are bid not to be afraid, for all these things, with all other are ordered, limited, enlarged and straitened, bounded and butted by the will, and hand, and power of that God unto whom Peter bids us commit the keeping of our souls, as unto a faithful Creator (verse 7-11; Mark 13:5-9). To wait for God in the way of his judgments doth well become a Christian.

To believe he loves us when he shows himself terrible to us, is also very much becoming of us. Wherefore has he given us grace? Is it that we should live by sense? Wherefore has he sometimes visited us? Is it that our hearts might be estranged from him, and that we still should love the world? And I say again, wherefore has he so plainly told us of his greatness, and of what he can do? Is it not that we might be still when the world is disturbed; and that we might hope for good things to come out of such providences that, to sense, look as if themselves would eat up and devour all?

Let us wait upon God, walk with God, believe in God, and commit ourselves, our soul, our body, to God, to be kept. Yea, let us be content to be at the disposal of God, and rejoice to see him act according to all his wondrous works. For this is a posture highly becoming them that say of God he is their Father, and that have committed the keeping of their souls to him as unto a Creator. A comely thing it is for the soul that feareth God, to love and reverence him in all his appearances. We should be like the spaniel dog, even lie at the foot of our God, as he at the foot of his master;

yea, and should be glad, could we but see his face, though he treads us down with his feet.

Ay, says one son, so I could, if I thought this high God would regard me, and take notice of my laying of my soul at his foot, while I suffer for his Word and truth in the world. Why, do but see now how the Holy Ghost, for our help, doth hedge up that way in at which unbelief would come, that there might, as to this, be no room left for doubting. For as he calleth the God unto whom we are bid to commit the keeping of our soul, a Creator, so he saith that he is A CREATOR THAT IS FAITHFUL. "Let them commit the keeping of their souls unto him in well-doing, as unto a faithful Creator"—a Creator that will concern himself with the soul committed to his trust, and that will be faithful to it, according to all that he has promised.

This, therefore, of God's faithfulness being added to his might and power, is in itself a ground of great support to those that have in a way of well-doing committed themselves, their souls, to him to keep. A Creator; what is it that a Creator cannot do? A faithful Creator; what is it that one that is faithful will not do, that is, when he is engaged? And now he is engaged, because thou hast committed thy soul to him to keep, and because he has bid thee do so. Let them commit the keeping of their soul to him, as unto a faithful Creator. I have sometimes seen an unfaithful man engaged, when a thing has been committed to him to keep. A man that is a thief, a cheater, a defrauder, will yet be faithful to him that will commit a charge to him to keep. And the reason is, because, though he can steal, cheat, defraud, without being taken notice of; yet he must be seen and known, if he be false in that which is committed to him to keep. I know the comparison is odious, yet such have been made by a holier mouth than mine, and as the case may be, they may be aptest of all to illustrate that which a man is about to explain. Hark what the unjust judge saith, says the Lord Jesus Christ (Luke 18).

To commit thy soul to God is to trust him with it; to commit thy soul to God is to engage him to look to it. And if he should not be faithful now, he will not be so in any case. For himself has bidden thee do it; he has also promised to keep it, as has been already showed in the former part of this discourse. Besides, he is here said to be faithful—to be a faithful Creator. He challenges this of faithfulness to himself alone: "Yea, let God be true, but every man a liar" (Rom 3:4). This, therefore, doth still help to encourage them that would be faithful to him, to commit the keeping of our soul to him. A faithful man will encourage one much; how much more should the faithfulness of God encourage us?

Here, therefore, we have a closing word indeed; a word to wrap up the text with that is as full of good as the sun is of light. What can be fitter spoken? What can be added? What now is wanting to the help of him that has committed his soul to God to keep it while he is suffering according to his will in the world? He is engaged, as I said, by that act; thou hast committed thy soul to him to keep; he is engaged by his own Word; he has bidden thee commit thy soul to him to keep. He is engaged by his declaring of himself to be faithful; for that has encouraged thee to commit thy soul to him to keep. Besides, he has promised to do it; he has sworn to do it.

"For when God made promise to Abraham, because he could swear by no greater, he sware by himself, saying, Surely blessing I will bless thee, and multiplying I will multiply thee. And so, after he had patiently endured, (as thou must do,) he obtained the promise. For men verily swear by the great: and an oath for confirmation is to them an end of all strife. Wherein God, willing more abundantly to shew unto the heirs of promise the immutability of his counsel, confirmed it by an oath: that by two immutable things, in which it was impossible for God to lie, we might have a strong consolation, who have fled for refuge to lay hold upon the hope set before us: which hope we have as an anchor of the soul, both sure and steadfast, and which entereth into that within the veil; whither the forerunner is for us entered, even Jesus, made an High-priest for ever after the order of Melchisedec" (Heb 6:13-20).

Thus you see what ground we have who suffer according to the will of God, and that have committed the keeping of our souls to him in well-doing, as unto a faithful Creator. Here, therefore, I might make a stop and conclude as to this advice; but now we are in, we will proceed a little further, and will fall upon three or four more particulars.

First, then, He will be faithful to us in this: He will keep us from those allurements of the world that a suffering saint is subject to. They that suffer have other kinds of temptations upon this account than other Christians have. The liberty of others, while they are in bonds, is a temptation to them. The peace of others, while they are in trouble, is a temptation to them. The enjoyments of others, while their houses are empty and their goods taken away, while their own water is sold unto them, and while they are buying their own wood, is a great temptation to them (Lam 5:4). And this temptation, were it not that we have to do with a God that is faithful, would assuredly be a great snare unto them. But "God is faithful, who will not suffer you to be tempted," as to this, "above that ye are able" (1 Cor 10:13).

Nay, a suffering man has not only these things lying before him as a temptation, but perhaps the wife of the bosom lies at him, saying, O do not cast thyself away; if thou takest this course, what shall I do? Thou has said thou lovest me; now make it manifest by granting this my small request. Do not still remain in thine integrity. Next to this come the children, all which are like to come to poverty, to beggary, to be undone for want of wherewithal to feed, and clothe, and provide for them for time to come. Now also come kindred, and relations, and acquaintance; some chide, some cry, some argue, some threaten, some promise, some flatter, and some do all, to befool him for so unadvised an act as to cast away himself, and to bring his wife and children to beggary for such a thing as religion. These are sore temptations.

Next to those come the terrors of men, the gripes of the laws, the shadow of death, and no man can tell what. All which are sufficient to pull a man from the gates of life, were he there, if the faithful Creator stands not to him. "But God is faithful, who will not suffer you to be tempted above that ye are able; but will with the temptation make a way to escape, that ye may be able to bear it."—"But God is faithful." It saith not, that thou art: but "God is faithful"—to his Son, to whom he has given thee; to his promise, the which he has given thee; to his cause, to which he has called thee; and to thy soul, the which thou hast committed to his trust, and the which he also has taken the charge of, as he is a faithful Creator.

"And will not suffer thee to be tempted." How, not tempted? No; not above what thou art able. He that tempts thee doth not at all consider thy strength, so as to stop when he sees thou art weak; he would have thee overthrown, for therefore it is that he tempteth thee. But God will not suffer that, because he is faithful, and because thou hast committed the keeping of thy soul unto him in well-doing, as unto a faithful Creator. "Not tempted above that ye are able." He saith not, above that ye are well able. Indeed, thy strength shall be proportioned to the temptation, but thou mayest have none over and above to spare; thou shalt not have a bigger load than God will give thee shoulders to bear. Christ did bear his burden, but it made him cry out, and sweat as it were great drops of blood, to carry it. Bear thy burden thou shalt, and not be destroyed by it; but perhaps thou mayest sometimes roar under it by reason of the disquietness of thy heart. "But he will with the temptation make a way of escape." "With the temptation," not without it; thou must be tempted, and must escape too. "With the temptation." As sure as Satan is licensed, so sure he is limited; and when Satan has ended all the temptation, he shall depart from thee (Luke 4:13). "He will with the temptation"—by such a managing of it as shall beak its own neck. God can admit Satan to tempt, and make the Christian wise to manage the temptation for his own escape.

"Make a way." It may be thou seest no way of escape. It may be there is no way—no way in all the world, to escape. Well; but God can make a way. When Israel was hemmed in at the Red Sea, there was as then no way—no way in all the world, to escape. O! but God made a way, and a pathway too, and that through the mighty waters (Exo 15:8,16; Psa 106:9; 78:13). He will make a way with the temptation, or "will with the temptation make a way to escape, that ye may be able to bear it." These are the words of the Holy Ghost, who is God; and they are spoken, yea, committed to record for this very purpose, that those that are under affliction might commit the keeping of their soul to him in well-doing, as unto a faithful Creator. That is the first.

Second, He will also be faithful to us as to this: He will give us a competent measure of wisdom, that in our suffering condition we may in all things be made able to manage our state with discretion. We are perhaps weak of natural abilities, parts of utterance, or the like; and our adversaries are learned, eloquent, and ripe of parts. Thou hast the disadvantage on thy side, and they have what the world can afford to encourage them; thou art weak of spirit, they are bold and strong. The great and the mighty are with thy enemies, but on thy side there is no comforter (Eccl 4:1).

Why now here is, as to this, and to what else can it be objected, the faithfulness of God engaged. First, in a general promise; I will not fail thee, nor forsake thee (Heb 13:5,6). Secondly, we have an invitation to come to this faithful God for wisdom to assist and help. For after he had said, "My brethren, count it all joy when ye fall into divers temptations - and let patience have her perfect work"; he adds, "If any man lack wisdom, let him ask of God, that giveth to all men liberally, and upbraideth not, and it shall be given him" (James 1:2-5). Here is more than an invitation, here is a promise—it shall be given him; and all to show us what a faithful Creator we have committed our souls unto. Doth any lack wisdom to know how to carry it in a time of trial: let them ask it of God—of the God that is wisdom itself; let him ask it of God, the liberal giver, who giveth to all men all that they have, and upbraideth not for their unworthiness.

Nor doth the Holy Ghost stop here, but enlarges himself in a more particular way to those that suffer according to the text, saying, "But when they deliver you up, take no thought how or what ye shall speak: for it shall be given you in that same hour what ye shall speak" (Matt 10:19). I have often been amazed in my mind at this text, for how could Jesus Christ have said such a word if he had not been able to perform it? This text, therefore, declares him to be God. It is also a proof of faithfulness to those that suffer for him.

For it is as if he should say, Try me and trust me; if I stand not by you in a day of distress, never believe me more;—you, suffering according to the will of God, and committing your souls to him in well-doing; "I will give you a mouth and wisdom, which all your adversaries shall not be able to gainsay or resist," for so he has it in Luke 21:15. Here is no consideration of what capacity the people might be of, that were to be persecuted; but what matters what they are? if fools, it is no matter; if wise, it helpeth nothing. A mouth and wisdom is to be given; that of itself shall do. And this is according to that other scripture mentioned afore, where it saith, "No weapon that is formed against thee shall prosper; and every tongue that shall rise against thee in judgment thou shalt condemn" (Isa 54:17). Although it may happen in this, as in the former temptation, the devil and his agents may give the saints, in their pleading for the truth, their bellies full both of cross answers, equivocations, sophistications, wrong glosses and erroneous interpretations; but truth shall prevail, shall turn the scale, and bear away the victory.

Third, He will also be faithful to us in this: we shall not want spiritual support to help us to bear up under our particular parts of suffering. I do not say that thou shalt be comforted all the while; but I say he will be to thee so faithful as to comfort thee under those thodes, gusts, blasts, or battering storms that beat against thy wall (Isa 32:2).

Look then what present degrees or aggravating appearances are in thy afflictions; to such a degree shalt thou at times be supported. For as surely as ever the Spirit of God moved Samson at times in the camp of Dan, when he lay against the Philistines; so will the Spirit of God move in and upon thee to comfort and to strengthen thee, whilst thou sufferest for his name in the world. As our afflictions abound for Christ, so shall our consolations abound by him (2 Cor 1:5). I have observed that God lays this, that he useth to comfort his people in a time of sufferings, as an aggravation of sin upon them that did use to shuck and shrink under sufferings. "I," saith he, "even I, am he that comforteth you; who art thou that thou shouldest be afraid of a man that shall die" (Isa 51:12)?

"God," says the wise man, "hath set the one over against the other," the day of adversity and the day of prosperity, "to the end that man should find nothing after him" to complain of (Eccl 7:14). For as certainly as there is a time to mourn, so certainly there is a time to rejoice: set, I say, for them that suffer for God's cause according to God's will (Eccl 3:4).

There are several degrees of suffering for righteousness; there is the scourge of the tongue, the ruin of an estate, the loss of liberty, a jail, a gibbet, a stake, a dagger. Now, answerable to these are the comforts of the Holy Ghost prepared, like to like, part proportioned to part, only the consolations are said to abound (2 Cor 1).

But the lighter the sufferings are, the more difficult it is to judge of the comforts of the Spirit of God, for it is common for a man to be comfortable under sufferings when he suffereth but little, and knows also that his enemy can touch his flesh, his estate, or the like, but little: I say, it is common for such a man to be comfortable in his sufferings, from the consideration that his enemies can touch him no further. And this may be the joy of the flesh—the result of reason, and may be very much, if not altogether, without a mixture of the joy of the Holy Ghost therewith. The more deep, therefore, and the more dreadful the sufferings are, the more clearly are seen the comforts of the Spirit, when a man has comfort where the flesh is dead, stirreth not, and can do nothing. When a man can be comfortable at the loss of all—when he is under the sentence of death, or at the place of execution—when a man's cause, a man's conscience, the promise, and the Holy Ghost, have all one comfortable voice, and do all, together with their trumpets, make one sound in the soul; then the comforts are good, of the right kinds, of God and his Spirit.

I told you before that there are several degrees of sufferings; wherefore it is not to be expected that he that suffers but little should partake of the comforts that are prepared for them that suffer much. He that has only the scourge of the tongue, knows not what are the comforts that are prepared for him that meets with the scourge of the whip. And how should a man know what manner of comforts the Holy Ghost doth use to give at the jail and the gibbet, when himself, for righteousness, never was there?

But whether this or the other Christian knows it, God has his consolations for his suffering people; and those, too, such as are proportioned to the nature or degree of their sufferings; the which shall assuredly be made appear to them that shall after a godly manner stick to his truth, and trust him with their souls. Joseph was cast into prison; but God was with him. John was banished into the isle called Patmos, for the Word of God; but what revelations of God had he there! even such as he was a stranger to all his life before: this, therefore, is to be well heeded. For it is a demonstration of the faithfulness of God to those that, suffering according to his will, do commit the keeping of their souls to him in well-doing, as unto a faithful Creator.

Fourth, He will also be faithful to us in this: He will not let the sharpness, nor keenness, nor venom of the arrows of the enemies of his people, reach so far as to destroy both body and soul at once; but he will preserve them, when what can be done is done, to his eternal kingdom and glory, is a marvellous thing; but it must be so, because God has called them to it. Therefore, after Peter had told them that the devil their adversary sought to devour them, and had bidden them resist him, steadfast in the faith, he saith, "But the God of all grace, who hath called us unto his eternal [kingdom and] glory by Christ Jesus, after that ye have suffered a while, make you perfect, stablish, strengthen, settle you" (1 Peter 5:10).
The truth is, persecution of the godly was, of God, never intended for their destruction, but for their glory, and to make them shine the more when they are beyond this valley of the shadow of death. Indeed, we ofttimes, when we are persecuted, do feel the terrors of our adversaries in our minds. But it is not because they can shoot them thither, nor because they of themselves have power to reach so far, but we, like fools, by our ignorance and unbelief, do admit them thither.

No suffering, nor inflicter of suffering, can reach the peace of the sufferer without his own consent. This is provision of God's making; yea, and if through our folly their terror is admitted to touch us, yet since we are not our own, but are bought with a price, we are not so at our own dispose, but that God will have the butting and bounding of their rage, as also a power to uphold and support our spirits. When I said my foot slipped, thy mercy, O Lord, help me up. And the reason why, by God's ordinance, the spirit is not to be touched in suffering, is, because that is it that is to sustain the infirmity of the sufferer; therefore God will have the spirit of his servants kept sound, and in good health (Prov 18:14; Isa 57:16). The room, therefore, and the ground that the enemy has to play upon, is the body and outward substance of the people of God, but the spirit is reserved, for the reason hinted before, and also that it might be capable of maintaining of communion with God. And how else could they obey that command that bids them rejoice in tribulation, and glorify God in the fires? as it is (Rom 12; Isa 24:15).

But, I say, if they have not power to touch, much less to destroy body and soul for ever. The body is God's, and he gives that to them to destroy; the spirit is God's, and he keeps that to himself, to show that he has both power to do with us what he pleases, and that he will recover our body also out of their hand; for if the spirit lives, so must the body, when men have done what they can therewith. This is the argument of our Lord Jesus Christ himself (Luke 20:37,38). Therefore the faithfulness of God not only is, but also will be seen, by them that dare trust him, till the next world, to his glory and their eternal comfort.

We will now conclude with a short word by way of USE. You see how I have opened the text, and what hath naturally followed thereupon; from the whole of which may be gathered:—

Use First, That the people of God are a suffering people—a people subject to trouble for their faith and profession. The reason is, besides what hath been said already, because the power of truth is in their hearts, and shows itself in their lives— a thing which the devil and the world can by no means abide. He that is born after the flesh persecuteth him that is born after the Spirit (Gal 4:29). For they cannot agree in religion; the godly are so devout and the other are so profane, that they cannot do. Not but that God's people, as they are commanded, are willing to let them alone; but the other they cannot bear that they should serve God as they have said (Matt 15:14), and hence ariseth persecution. The world also would have the religion of the godly to be counted false—a thing that the others can by no means endure, but will stand by and maintain, yet in all peaceable manner, their own ways before them, whatever it costs.

The Christian and the carnal professor are like those two harlots that you read of in the book of Kings, who strove for the living child, whose it should be, whose contest could not be decided until it came to the sword of the king (1 Kings 3). O, but when the sword was drawn, under a show as if the living child must now be cut in two, then the true mother was known from the false; for her bowels yearned upon her son (verse 26,27). The world, what show soever they have for religion, and however they urge it, that the truth is with them, have no yearning of bowels for it. Let it be neither mine nor thine, said she, but divide it; but the woman whose the living child was, had not a heart to say so. Religion may lie and die in a ditch for all those that are given to their sins; nor doth their zeal appear, except when they are gripping of the godly for his faith towards God. Bowels, yearning of bowels over God's condemned religion, is only found in the souls of those who own God has made it.

Use Second, Is it so? Are God's people a suffering people? Then this should inform them that will be religious, to prepare themselves for what is like to attend them for their religion. To prepare, I say, not with carnal weapons, but with the graces of the Spirit of God; that will help them with meekness and patience to endure. Sit down then, I say, and count up the cost, before for religion thou engagest too far; lest thou take upon thee to meddle with that which thou wilt not know what to do with in the end (Prov 25:8; Luke 14:25-30).

Many there be that are faulty here; they have taken upon them to profess, not considering what they have taken in hand may cost them. Wherefore, when troubles come indeed, then they start and cry. This they like not, because they looked not for it; and if this be the way to heaven, let who will go on in it for them. Thus they take offence, and leave Christ's cause and people to shift for themselves in the world (Matt 13:20,21).

Use Third, But let God's people think never the worse of religion, because of the coarse entertainment it meeteth with in the world. It is better to choose God and affliction than the world, and sin, and carnal peace. It is necessary that we should suffer, because that we have sinned. And if God will have us suffer a little while here for his Word, instead of suffering for our sins in hell, let us be content, and count it a mercy with thankfulness.

"The wicked is reserved to the day of destruction: they shall be brought forth to the day of wrath" (Job 21:30). How kindly, therefore, doth God deal with us, when he chooses to afflict us but for a little, that with everlasting kindness he may have mercy upon us (Isa 54:7,8). And "it is better, if the will of God be so, that ye suffer for well-doing than for evil-doing" (1 Peter 3:17).

Use Fourth, Look not, therefore, upon the sufferings of God's people for their religion, to be tokens of God's great anger. It is, to be sure, as our heavenly Father orders it, rather a token of his love; for suffering for the gospel, and for the sincere profession of it, is indeed a dignity put upon us—a dignity that all men are not counted worthy of. Count it, therefore, a favour that God has bestowed upon thee his truth, and graces to enable thee to profess it, though thou be made to suffer for it (Acts 5:41). Thou mightest have been a sufferer for thy sins in hell, but thou art not; but contrariwise art, perhaps, suffering for conscience to God; this is a dignity. For that thou dost thus by virtue of a heavenly gift, on the behalf of Christ, for the gospel's sake, and according to the will of God. This is a dignity that a persecutor shall not be counted worthy of, until he first convert to Christ (Phil 1:29).

Use Fifth, Take thy affliction with meekness and patience, though thou endurest grief wrongfully. "For this is thankworthy, if a man for conscience toward God endure grief, suffering wrongfully" (1 Peter 2:19). Lay thy hand, then, upon thy mouth, and speak not a word of ill against him that doth thee wrong; leave thy cause and thy enemy to God; yea, rather pray that his sin may not be laid to his charge; wherefore, as I said before, now show thyself a good man, by loving, pitying, praying for, and by doing good, as thou art commanded, to them that despitefully use thee (Matt 5:44). I know thy flesh will be apt to huff, and to be angry, and to wish, would thou mightest revenge thyself. But this is base, carnal, sensual, devilish; cast, therefore, such thoughts from thee, as thoughts that are not fit for a Christian's breast, and betake thee to those weapons that are not carnal. For the artillery of a Christian is the Word, faith, and prayer; and in our patience we must possess our souls (2 Cor 10:5; Luke 21:16-19).

Use Sixth, Be much in the consideration of the all-sufficiency of thy Father, whose cause thou hast espoused, whose Word thou hast chosen for thy heritage, and whose paths thou delightest to walk in. I say, be much in considering how all the world is sustained by him, and that all life and breath is in his hand, to continue or diminish as he pleases. Think with thyself also how able he is to rescue thee from all affliction, or to uphold thee in it with a quiet mind. Go to him continually, as to a fountain of life that is open for the supply of the needy. Remember also, if he comes not at thy call, and comforteth thee not so soon as thou desirest, it is not of want of love or compassion to thy soul, but to try thy graces, and to show to the fallen angels that thou wilt serve God for nought, rather than give out. Also, if it seemeth to thee, as if God took no care of thee to help thee, but that he hath rather turned thee over to the ungodly; count this also as a sign that he delights to see thee hold fast his name, though thou art laid under the greatest of disadvantages. "If the scourge slay suddenly, [that is more than it hath done to thee,] he will laugh at the trial of the innocent" (Job 9:23).

It is a great delight to our God to see his people hold fast their integrity, and not to deny his name, when under such cloudy dispensations and discouraging circumstances. And considerations that thy thus doing is pleasing in his sight through Christ, will be a support unto thee. God sees thee, though thou canst not now see him, and he observeth now thy way, though darkness is round about him; and when he hath tried thee, thou shalt come forth like gold.

Use Seventh, Take heed of setting of thyself a bound and period to thy sufferings, unless that period be the grave. Say not to thy afflicters, Hitherto, and no further, and here shall your proud waves be stayed. I say, take heed of doing thus, for fear God should let them go beyond thee. For a man is not prepared to suffer, further than he thinketh the enemy may be permitted to go. Hence Christ sets their bounds at the loss of life, and no nearer. So then, so far as they go beyond thee, so far they will find thee unprovided, and so not fortified for a reception of their onset with that Christian gallantry which becomes thee. Observe Paul; he died daily, he was always delivered unto death, he despaired of life; and this is the way to be prepared for any calamity. When a man thinks he has only to prepare for an assault by footmen, how shall he contend with horses? Or if he looks no further than to horses, what will he do at the swellings of Jordan (Jer 12:5)? Wherefore, set thine enemies no bounds: say not, They shall not pursue me to the death; have the sentence of death in thyself. For though they may but tick and toy with thee at first, their sword may reach thy heart-blood at last. The cat at play with the mouse is sometimes a fit emblem of the way of the wicked with the children of God. Wherefore, as I said, be always dying; die daily: he that is not only ready to be bound, but to die, is fit to encounter any amazement.

Use Eighth, If thine enemies would, or do, put thee under a cloud, if they wrap thee up in a bear's skin, and then set the dogs upon thee, marvel not at the matter; this was Joseph's, David's, Christ's, Stephen's portion, only be thou innocent; say nothing, do nothing that should render thee faulty; yea, say and do always that that should render thee a good neighbour, a good Christian, and a faithful subject. This is the way to help thee to make with boldness thy appeals to God; this is the way to embolden thy face against the faces of thine enemies; this is the way to keep thy conscience quiet and peaceable within thee; and this is the way to provoke God to appear for thy rescue, or to revenge thy blood when thou art gone. And do this because it is thy duty—we must fear God and honour the king—and because this is the way to make the rock of thy enemies hard: few men have that boldness as to say, This I do against you, because you profess Christ. When they persecuted the Lord himself, they said to him, "For a good work we stone thee not" (John 10:33). Religion that is pure is a hot thing, and it usually burns the fingers of those that fight against it; wherefore it is not common for men to oppose religion under its own naked complexion: wherefore the Jews sought to fasten other matters upon Christ to kill him for them; though the great spite they had against him was for his doctrine and miracles. It was for envy to that that they set themselves against him, and that made them invent to charge him with rebellion and treason (Matt 27:18; Luke 23:2).

Use Ninth, Wherefore it becomes all godly men to study to be quiet, to mind their own business, and as much as in them lies, to be at peace with all men; to owe no man any thing but love. Pray, therefore, for all that are in authority; pray for the peace of the country in which thou dwellest; keep company with holy, and quiet, and peaceable men. Seek by all good ways the promotion of godliness, put up injuries, be good to the poor, do good against evil, be patient towards all men; for "these things are good and profitable unto men" (Titus 3:8).

Be not inclining to injure men behind their backs, speak evil of no man, reproach not the governor nor his actions, as he is set over thee; all his ways are God's, either for thy help or the trial of thy graces. Wherefore he needs thy prayers, not thy revilings; thy peaceable deportment, and not a troublesome life. I know that none of these things can save thee from being devoured by the mouth of the sons of Belial (1 Kings 21:12,13). Only, what I say is duty, is profitable, is commendable, is necessary; and that which will, when the devil has done his worst, render thee lovely to thy friends, terrible to thine enemies, serviceable in thy place as a Christian, and will crown the remembrance of thy name, to them that survive thee, with a blessing; "The memory of the just is blessed: but the name of the wicked shall rot" (Prov 10:7).

Use Tenth, I will conclude, then, with a word to those professors, if there be any such, that are of an unquiet and troublesome spirit. Friends, I may say to you, as our Lord said once to his disciples, "Ye know not what manner of spirit ye are of." To wish the destruction of your enemies doth not become you. If ye be born to, and are called, that you may inherit a blessing, pray be free of your blessing: "Bless, and curse not." If you believe that the God whom you serve is supreme governor, and is also wise enough to manage affairs in the world for his church, pray keep fingers off, and refrain from doing evil. If the counsel of Gamaliel was good when given to the enemies of God's people, why not fit to be given to Christians themselves? Therefore refrain from these men, and let them alone. If the work that these men do is that which God will promote and set up for ever, then you cannot disannul it; if not, God has appointed the time of its fall.

A Christian! and of a troublesome spirit; for-shame, forbear; show, out of a good conversation, thy works, with meekness of wisdom; and here let me present thee with three or four things.

1. Consider, That though Cain was a very murderer, yet God forbade any man's meddling with him, under a penalty of revenging his so doing upon his own head sevenfold. "And the Lord said

unto him, Therefore, whosoever slayeth Cain, vengeance shall be taken on him sevenfold" (Gen 4:15). But why not meddle with Cain, since he was a murderer? The reason is, because he persecuted his brother for righteousness' sake, and so espoused a quarrel against God; for he that persecutes another for righteousness' sake sets himself against God, fights against God, and seeks to overthrow him. Now, such an one the Christian must let alone and stand off from, that God may have his full blow at him in his time. Wherefore he saith to his saints, and to all that are forward to revenge themselves, Give place, stand back, let me come, leave such an one to be handled by me. "Dearly beloved, avenge not yourselves, but rather give place unto wrath; for it is written, Vengeance is mine, I will repay, saith the Lord" (Rom 12:19). Wherefore the Lord set a mark upon Cain, lest any finding him should slay him. You must not indeed, you must not avenge yourselves of your enemies. Yea, though it was lawful once so to do, it is not lawful now. Ye have heard that it hath been said to them of old time, Thou shalt love thy neighbour and hate thine enemy; but I say, said our Lord, Love them, bless them, do good to them, and pray for them that hate you (Matt 5:43,44).

2. Consider, Revenge is of the flesh,—I mean this our revenge of ourselves; and it proceeds from anger, wrath, impatience under the cross, unwillingness to suffer, from too much love to carnal ease, to estates, to enjoyments, to relations, and the like. It also flows from a fearful, cowardly spirit; there is nothing of greatness in it, except it be greatness of untowardness. I know there may, for all this, be pretences to justice, to righteousness, to the liberty of the gospel, the suppressing of wickedness, and the promoting of holiness; but these can be but pretences, or, at best, but the fruits of a preposterous zeal. For since, as has been often said in this treatise, the Lord hath forbidden us to do so, it cannot be imagined that he should yet animate any to such a thing by the Holy Ghost and the effects of the graces thereof. Let them, then, if any such be, that are thus minded, be counted the narrow-spirited, carnal, fleshly, angry, waspish-spirited professors—the professors that know more of the Jewish than of the Christian religion, and that love rather to countenance the motions, passions, and gross motions of and angry mind, that with meekness to comply with the will of a heavenly Father. Thou art bid to be like unto him, and also thou art showed wherein (Matt 5:45-48).

There is a man hates God, blasphemes his name, despises his being; yea, says there is no God. And yet the God that he carrieth it thus towards doth give him his breakfast, dinner, and supper; clothes him well, and when night comes, has him to bed, gives him good rest, blesses his field, his corn, his cattle, his children, and raises him to high estate. Yea, and this our God doth not only once or twice, but until these transgressors become old; his patience is thus extended, years after years, that we might learn of him to do well.

3. Consider, A professor! and unquiet and troublesome, discontented, and seeking to be revenged of thy persecutors; where is, or what kind of grace hast thou got? I dare say, they, even these in which thou thus actest, are none of the graces of the Spirit. The fruits of the Spirit are love, joy,

peace, long- suffering, gentleness, goodness, faith, meekness, temperance; against such there is no law; but wrath, strife, seditions, traitors, and inventors of evil things are reckoned with the worst of sins, and sinners, and are plainly called the works of the flesh (Rom 1:29-31; 2 Tim 3:3,4; Gal 5:19-21).

But I say, where is thy love to thine enemy? where is thy joy under the cross? where is thy peace when thine anger has put thee upon being unquiet? Where is thy long-suffering? for, as thou actest, not ought but thy waspishness can be seen. Where, also, is thy sweet, meek, and gentle spirit? and is goodness seen in thy seeking the life or the damage of thy enemy? Away, away; thy graces, if thou hast any, are by these, thy passions, so jostled up into corners, and so pent for want of room and liberty to show themselves, that, by the Word of God, thou canst not be known to be of the right kind, what a noise soever thou makest.

A Christian, when he sees trouble coming upon him, should not fly in the face of the instrument that brings it, but in the face of the cause of its coming. Now the cause is thyself, thy base self, thy sinful self, and thy unworthy carriages towards God under all the mercy, patience, and long-suffering that God has bestowed upon thee, and exercised towards thee. Here thou mayest quarrel and be revenged, and spare not, so thou take vengeance in a right way, and then thou wilt do so when thou takest it by godly sorrow (2 Cor 7:10,11).

A Christian, then, should bewail his own doings, his own unworthy doings, by which he has provoked God to bring a cloud upon him, and to cover him with it in anger. A Christian should say, This is my wickedness, when a persecutor touches him; yea, he should say it, and then shut up his mouth, and bear the indignation of the Lord, because he has sinned against him. "Thy way and thy doings have procured these things unto thee; this is thy wickedness, because it is bitter, because it reacheth unto thine heart" (Jer 4:18).

4. Consider, What conviction of thy goodness can the actions that flow from such a spirit give unto observers? None at all; yea, a spirit of unquietness under sufferings, and that seeketh to be revenged of those that do, for thy faith and the profession thereof, persecute thee, is so far off of giving conviction to beholders that thou art right, that it plainly tells them that thou art wrong. Even Julian the apostate, when he had cast away whatever he could of Christ, had this remaining with him—that a Christian ought to take with patience what affliction fell upon him for his Master's sake; and would hit them in the teeth with an unbecoming behavior, that complained or that sought redress of them that had abused them for their faith and godly profession. What will men say if you shrink and winch, and take your sufferings unquietly, but that if you yourselves were uppermost, you would persecute also? Much more have they ground to say so, when you will fight lying on your backs. Be quiet, then, and if thine enemy strike thee on one check, turn to him the other; and if he also revile and curse thee, down upon thy knees and pray for him. This is the way to convince thy observers that thou art a godly man. Father, forgive them, for they know

not what they do, was one of those things that convinced the centurion that Jesus was a righteous man; for he stood by the cross to watch and see how Jesus carried it in these his sufferings, as well as to see execution done (Matt 27:54; Luke 23:34-47).

5. Consider, A professor, unquiet and turbulent under sufferings, and seeking his own revenge, cannot be a victor over what he should, nor a keeper of God's commandments.

(1.) How can he be a victor over himself that is led up and down by the nose by his own passions? There is no man a Christian victor but he that conquers himself, but he that beats down and keeps under this body, his lusts, his passions, in the first place. He he that is led away with them more a victor? Is he that is a servant to corruption a victor? And if he that is captivated by his anger, wrath, passion, discontent, prejudice, &c., be not led away by them, I am under a mistake. So then, to quarrel with superiors, or with any that are troublesome to thee for thy faith and thy profession, bespeaks thee over-mastered and captive, rather than a master and a conqueror.

(2.) The same may be said upon the second head. He keepeth not the commandments of God; for those teach him other things, as I have also showed. The great gospel commands terminate in self-denial; but if self-revenge is self-denial, I am besides the Book. Christ, in the book of the Revelation, sets him that keeps the commandments of God a great way off from him that taketh and smiteth with the sword: "He that killeth with the sword must be killed with the sword. Here is the patience and the faith of the saints" (Rev 13:10). That is, in that they forbear to do thus, and quietly suffer under those that thus take it and afflict the godly with it. Again, "Here is the patience of the saints, here are they that keep the commandments of God and the faith of Jesus" (14:12). A patient continuing in well- doing; and if suffering for righteousness be well-doing, then a patient continuing in that, as in other things, is the way to keep God's commandments (Rom 2:7).

So that, I say, he keepeth not God's commandments that is angry with his enemies, and that seeks to be revenged of him that doth him ill. You know the subject I am upon. "The wrath of man worketh not the righteousness of God" (James 1:20). Wherefore, professors, beware, and take heed to your spirits, and see that you let not out yourselves under your sufferings in such extravagancies of spirit against your enemies as is no way seemly nor convenient.

6. Consider, Men that are unquiet and discontented, and that seek revenge upon them that persecute them for their profession, do, by so doing, also put themselves upon the brink of those ruins that others are further from. These men are like the fly that cannot let the candle alone until she hath burned herself in the flame. Magistrates and men in power have fortified themselves from being attacked with turbulent and unruly spirits by many and wholesome laws. And, indeed, should they not do so, one or other, perhaps, would be quickly tempted to seek to disturb

them in the due exercise of their authority. Now the angry man, he is the fly that must be tripping and running himself upon the point of these laws; his angry spirit puts him upon quarrelling with his superiors, and his quarrelling brings him, by words spoke in heat, within the reach of the net, and that, with the help of a few more, brings his neck to the halter. Nor is this, whatever men think, but by the just judgment of God. "Whosoever, therefore, resisteth the power, resisteth the ordinance of God; and they that resist shall receive to themselves damnation" (Rom 13:2; Esth 2:21-23). Wherefore, let the angry man take heed; let the discontented man take heed. He that has a profession, and has not grace to know, in this matter, to manage it, is like to bring his profession to shame. Wherefore, I say, let such take heed; and the graces afore mentioned, and the due exercise of them, are they and that which can keep us out of all such dangers.

7. Consider, And what comfort can such a man have who has, by his discontent and unruly carriages, brought himself, in this manner, to his end; he has brought himself to shame, his profession to shame, his friends to shame, and his name to contempt and scorn. Bad men rejoice at his fall; good men cannot own him, weak men stumble at him; besides, his cause will not bear him out; his heart will be clogged with guilt; innocency and boldness will take wings and fly from him. Though he talketh of religion upon the stage or ladder, that will blush to hear its name mentioned by them that suffer for evil-doing. Wherefore, my brethren, my friends, my enemies, and all men, what religion, profession, or opinion soever you hold, fear God, honour the king, and do that duty to both which is required of you by the Word and law of Christ, and then, to say no more, you shall not suffer by the power for evil-doing.

Made in the USA
Middletown, DE
17 December 2020